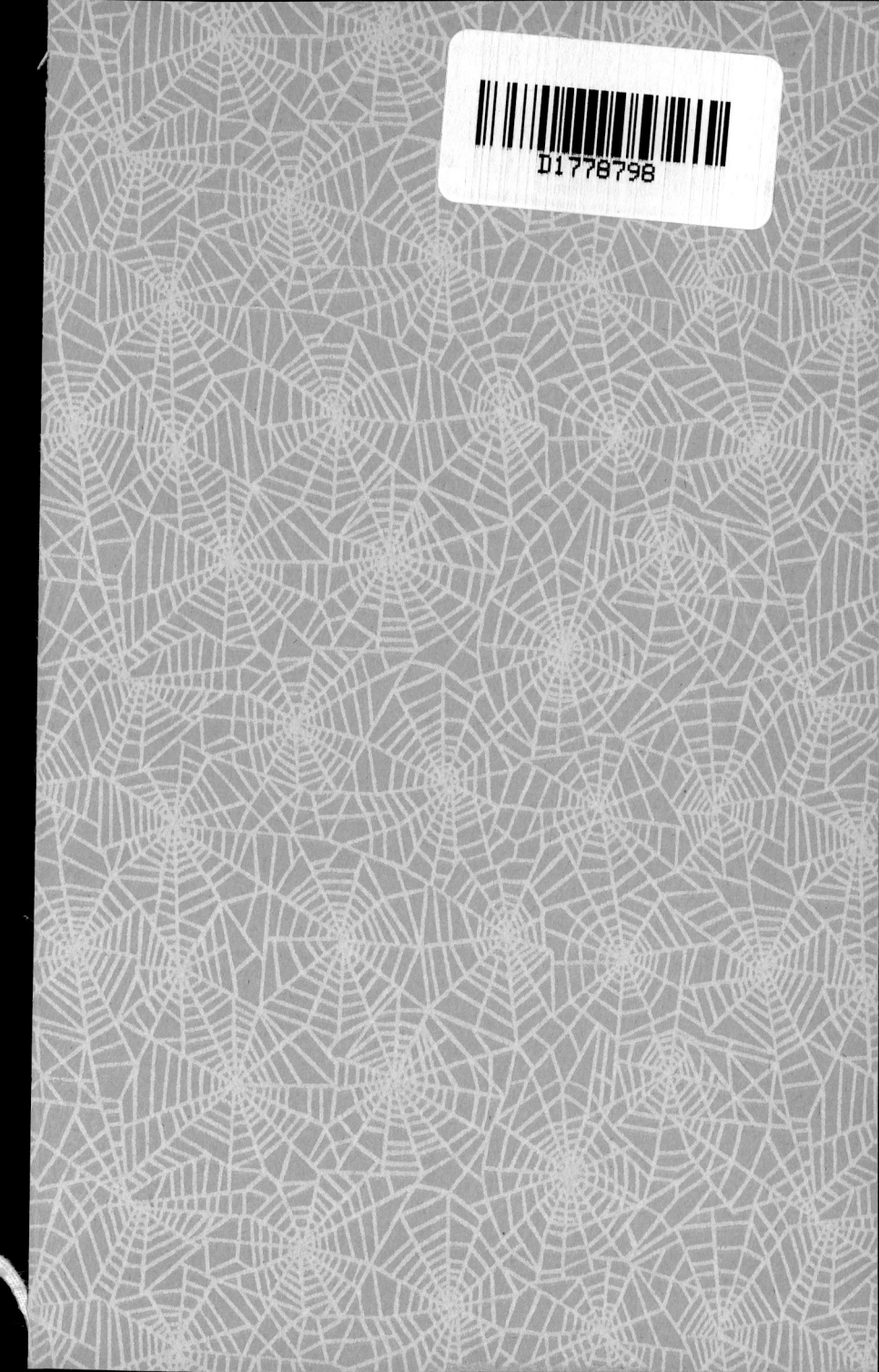

BEYOND PLEDGING

AN INFORMAL GUIDE TO LAY LEADERSHIP IN THE EPISCOPAL CHURCH

INTRODUCTION BY
Oscar C. Carr, Jr.

BEYOND PLEDGING

Charles R. Supin

A CROSSROAD BOOK

The Seabury Press / New York

The Seabury Press
815 Second Avenue
New York, N.Y. 10017

Copyright © 1974 by Development Office, the Executive Council of the Episcopal Church
Designed by S. S. Drate
Printed in the United States of America

All rights reserved. No part of this book may be reproduced in any manner whatsoever without written permission from the publisher, except for brief quotations contained in critical reviews and articles.

LIBRARY OF CONGRESS CATALOGING IN PUBLICATION DATA

Supin, Charles R.
  Beyond pledging.

  "A Crossroad book."
  1. Laity—Anglican Communion. I. Title.
BX5968.S9   262'.15   74-12315
ISBN 0-8164-2108-0

Contents

Introduction *by Oscar C. Carr, Jr.*   vii

PART ONE
One View from the Pew

A. *The Calling*   3
B. *The Renewal Committee*   17
C. *Assessment and Renewal*   35

PART TWO
The Overview

A. *The Diocese*   83
B. *The General Church Program*   149
C. *Impressions*   165

Notes   169

Introduction

> In order for an idea to change the world it must change the
> life of the man who carries it. It must become an example.
> —Albert Camus

Twenty minutes before adjournment of the 63rd General Convention in Houston, Texas in 1970, a deputy from the Diocese of New York introduced a resolution proposing an Office of Development for the Episcopal Church. It was seconded by a deputy from the Diocese of the Rio Grande and passed both Houses without debate.

It was a desperation vote, cast with almost blind faith, in the waning moments of a frustrating convention. In fact, it was voted with so much faith that the accompanying appropriation for the office was inadequate.

The Office of Development became a reality only when the Executive Council received a tithe from a Diocese of Rochester legacy which designated half of the fund to this Office. I resigned from the Executive Council on the first of September, 1971, to accept appointment by the Presiding Bishop as Vice President for Development of the Episcopal Church.

Why was the office created?

I believe that this was the way the Houston Convention decided to deal with its frustration, since it could not then respond adequately to the needs and opportunities confronting the church.

The Convention was simply unable to formulate a valid

case for support of a General Church Program to which the entire church would wholeheartedly and enthusiastically respond.

The Executive Council, in responding to the General Convention resolution creating the Office of Development, decided —wisely I am convinced—to tackle the problem head-on by *asking* the *right* questions. It decided that if we were to build a case for a General Church Program that could be supported enthusiastically by the church, then the *church must* have a significant role in shaping that Program.

The Office of Development was charged with the managerial role of this fact-finding effort.

After receiving approval and invitations from our diocesan bishops to visit their dioceses, we trained our visiting teams. One hundred and one team members, consisting of bishops, priests, deacons and lay persons (since known as the "Chicago 101"), hit the airways in teams of three—travelling 463,635 miles—a distance greater than eighteen circumventions of the earth—and in two months gathered grass-roots data from Hawaii to Maine, from Alaska to Arkansas. Twenty thousand people were consulted as to what they thought about the content of the General Church Program, the priorities for such a Program, and how it should be funded. This massive interrogation would have had no chance for success had it not been for the dedicated church leaders who joined a lesser number of elected Executive Council members and staff members to comprise the teams. Although far from perfect, the venture was a success because it involved church leaders of all descriptions, orders, and backgrounds working in a collaborative style.

The process had credibility, because it had integrity. The smooth transition of this data into a General Church Program and Budget adopted at the 64th General Convention at Louisville is now history.

There were many learnings from the massive interrogation of the Episcopal Church under the auspices of the Office of Development on which we need to continue to build. One learning was that there is a great lack of knowledge at the parish level about diocesan activities, the program of the church at the national and international level, and how they all relate. We found that there is relatively little material to help the average church member understand these matters. We also found many crying for resources in the area of "on-going stewardship."

Although there are excellent textbooks on the market covering the very specific work of fund raising and organizational development, they are for the most part dry and unexciting for the very person who needs them most.

Who is this person? He is the one called upon by rectors, bishops, and others to assume a new leadership role in the church—such as leading an Every Member Canvass, serving as a vestryman or officer of some guild, understanding something about the life and work of the church whether in a small church or a large diocese, or programs and policies carried on at the national level and beyond.

But what does *this* book try to do?

Through a central character not unlike many of the people to be found in the pew, the reader can discover different styles of leadership within the rigors of fund raising or simply keeping the ship afloat. In a painless and non-threatening way the reader can discover some new trends in organizational development, a technical subject one might not normally study otherwise. The dialogue offers the informality of experience. The absence of technical terminology and jargon makes it more readable.

This book is an informal approach to life on all levels of the Episcopal Church. *It assumes that the discovery of program—by setting objectives in advance—goes hand in hand with the methods of raising financial support.* This is what *development* is all about.

As the church seeks to develop talent on every level, this book can be an informative yet informal journey of discovery into this "family" we call the Episcopal Church.

The style in this narrative is light, but not superficial. It is written by one who loves the church, and one who wants to see the church approach its potential.

The author is the Rev. Charles Supin, graduate of Berkeley Divinity School, rector of a parish in the Diocese of Nevada, who was very helpful to me as Coordinator for Development during the period of our visits to the dioceses. We are grateful for Father Supin's efforts in preparing this book for the Office of Development.

Although none of us believes that this book will "change the world," we are convinced that it will be helpful for those in new leadership roles, and that it may "become an example" for other materials yet to come.

April, 1974

Oscar C. Carr, Jr.
Executive for Development/Stewardship
The Episcopal Church
New York City

Part One

ONE VIEW FROM THE PEW

A.
The Calling

INVITATION

Joe Joiner, the hero in this narrative, is a member of the Episcopal Church. That is to say, he has made a series of commitments: personal ties to the intangible and tangible, the spiritual and temporal. Until now, he has successfully managed to give this commitment a minimum of attention.

Joe's parents were always Episcopalians, as far as he knew, but they surely never took it very seriously. He vaguely remembers coloring Joseph's beard in endless classes in the church school, and receiving a potted plant or two at Easters long past. Sixteen years ago, Joe and his wife, Betty, were married in an Episcopal Church, mainly because it was the prettiest church in town. They have three children.

The Joiners have moved no less than four times in the last ten years, as Joe has pursued his career as an architect. They have passed through many towns, and as many parishes. They felt that joining a parish was always the right thing to do. However, they have gone through such a hectic succession of

4 BEYOND PLEDGING

campaigns for new hymnals, organ pipes, foreign missions, and cost of living increases that, since joining the parish in Goodplace, U.S.A., six months ago, they have resorted to slipping silently into the last pew during the final stanza of the processional. They preferred to be members of the parish from a safe distance.

But sure enough, no sooner did Joe kneel to pray, stand to sing, and sit to be instructed, on that particular Sunday, than the Rector, at the chancel steps, reminded him and the other worshipers that the boiler in the parish house was inoperable, the diocese wanted to open a drug-counseling facility, and the national church was thinking about a capital fund drive. With one hand Joe crushed the leaflet, with the other he squeezed Betty's hand. "Here we go again," he whispered.

At the door, the Rector squeezed Joe's hand and asked, "Mr. Joiner? Do you have time to meet with me in the parish house next Saturday morning?" Joe's mind was on lunch and the newspapers, so he nodded and said something to the effect that he'd be there at ten o'clock.

Not until hours later, after he had digested his pie and read the sports pages, did he realize what he had done. "Betty," he burst out to his wife, "do you know what I did at church this morning?"

His wife looked up from the editorial page, expecting all kinds of revelation.

"I gave up next Saturday's tennis doubles, that's what I did."

On Saturday Joe arrived at the parish house at ten o'clock. He wore his sports clothes as a reminder to himself and the Rector that sacrifice on the weekend was a multi-faceted concept. The Rector was waiting for him, silhouetted against a backdrop of walls in need of paint, grass in need of cutting, windows in need of washing, and a roof that had fought too many losing battles with the wind. Joe reassured himself that it couldn't possibly be one of those work days scheduled by some buildings and grounds committee, since there were just the two of them.

The Rector thanked him for coming on his day of leisure and, before Joe knew what was happening, he was ushered into the nave of the church, a dimly lit edifice which had been standing for fifty years. There was enough light to show that it was in need of tender loving strokes of a paint brush, if not a dust mop. The Rector paused in silence—while Joe wondered what in God's name he had gotten himself into.

The Rector was in his mid-fifties, married, with two children of college age. He started talking about this as he ushered Joe from the nave to the sacristy and through the corridor to the parish house. The Rector had been in this parish for eight years, had seen the membership rise then fall to where it was now forty percent less than when he came. Near the kitchen, which was in need of a new stove and dishes, the Rector told him that his personal salary had risen only one thousand dollars in the eight years; along with his wife's part-time income, it would be enough to cover most of the college bills. As they walked past the small and cluttered classrooms on one side of the parish house, the Rector confessed that his age probably precluded him from getting another position elsewhere, so he might very well be the Rector here for another fifteen years. By the time the Rector reached the broken-down boiler he confessed that the parish needed a shot in the spiritual arm, and that took leadership from the laity, and the man who was supposed to be a special leader this year had just been transferred to another town. Then came the question:

"Joe, would you help us by accepting the chairmanship of our Every Member Canvass?"

Money! Chairman of a fund-raising drive! Now he regretted wearing expensive sports clothes. Maybe they thought he was loaded. Wait until Betty heard about this!

The Rector, ushering Joe out the door to the parking lot, asked him not to answer at this time but, rather, would he be willing to come to the church office next Friday afternoon? Joe said fine, even though he felt sure that he would telephone his refusal by Wednesday.

By the time Joe was seated behind the wheel of his car, the Rector had admitted that he knew little about the characteristics of fund raising, never having studied the subject formally. Moreover, before moving away last week, the man who was supposed to be chairman had gathered some materials on leadership and organizational development which were available to Joe if he wanted them. Joe thanked the Rector and turned the ignition key (if he hurried he could still play a set or two). The motor jumped to life.

"Oh, there's just one more thing."

Joe tightened his grip on the steering wheel, and listened. The one more thing was a request by the Rector that they do a little homework before Friday. Both he and the Rector would answer two questions: what was good about the parish and what was bad about it. The Rector suggested it might be informative if they compared notes from a new member of the parish, and from one who might have been a member too long. Joe did not comment about that one, but agreed to make out the lists. After a couple of thank-yous, Joe drove out of the parking lot wondering if he would ever drive back in again.

On Sunday morning he stayed home from church to brood. What was it that the Rector really wanted? He had mentioned something about his salary increases, but nothing about the overall budget of the parish. Was it a sly pitch for a salary boost? Look, life was tough all over. Everyone had college bills or dentist bills or, sure, even tennis club bills. And Joe was not going to be intimidated just because he played tennis, and liked nice clothes.

Joe grew angrier with each new thought. He was no leader,

no organizer. Although there was something nice about being tapped by someone, because it meant that person thought you had something special to offer. But then, who needed the aggravation? Joe knew he had enough problems of his own. The Rector was paid—who cared how much—to do parish things. It was the Rector's problem. Joe concluded that church was a pain in the neck and, for relief, he turned to the travel section of the newspaper.

By Wednesday Joe Joiner had calmed down and was trying to figure out what the Rector had done to him the week before. First of all, the Rector had been candid, and brutally honest about himself. Moreover, he had given Joe a tour of the facilities. And what had Joe seen? Plenty of space, most of it in bad repair, and surely only partially used for very few hours each week. So, there were limitations, on one hand, and lots of potential, on the other hand. And, as was all too evident, not many hands doing anything about it.

Joe reached for two pieces of paper; on one he wrote GOOD at the top, and on the other, BAD. What was good about this parish? Well, it had a Rector who could pick leaders. But then again, could he? The buildings were a mess. The attendance seemed to be dropping steadily. They were in need of cash, and paint. The ushers didn't really care if Betty and he got there late for services on Sunday. He had failed to learn anything about the beliefs of the church. He did not know any of the members, really. His children were polite about the whole thing, but indifferent. Betty helped to arrange flowers on the altar, and made cookies on two occasions for the coffee hour, which they rarely attended. They took envelopes, and put in a check for three dollars whenever they attended worship. Joe supposed these were neither *good* nor *bad*, merely facts of life. He tore up the two pieces of paper, took two fresh ones, and tried to start again.

Joe thought about himself. He was a good architect with a

promising future. Like most of his friends, he was white, a suburbanite, fairly successful by the usual standards. His tennis club was not restricted. It merely catered to the people in the neighborhood. He had a comfortable home, bigger than the last one, and—if he watched the charge accounts—he had enough money to live reasonably well. Joe was neither an adulterer nor a gambler. He assumed he was well liked. Liked well enough to be tapped by the Rector of the local parish.

But the parish meant little to him. Until now, it had never occurred to him to wonder why. Isolated sermons about Indian children somewhere, or changes in The Book of Common Prayer, were not frequent enough to be bothersome. The bishop, who came for his son's Confirmation, looked the part, and said encouraging things about the Rector and the state of the worldwide Church; plus a reminder that he and his diocesan staff were willing to do anything that was needed on the local level, and his door was always open, but would they please telephone for an appointment first. No real problems there, as far as Joe could see.

Why, Joe asked himself, was the Episcopal Church losing members? He had been told that baptisms were down, fewer people were giving money, . . . But was it really his worry? Getting to worship on any regular basis was enough of a strain. Well, it wasn't really a strain, but, oh well, . . . It was not very important. It was downright dull.

For courtesy reasons only, Joe decided to meet with the Rector on Friday afternoon, but he thought it best not to bring the pieces of paper listing what was good and bad. He would play it by ear, and close to his chest.

DISCOVERY

The Rector was obviously pleased that Joe was willing to meet with him. "After three years of seminary," the Rector reminded him, "I was ordained and thrust into an executive role without the training or on-the-job experiences." He added that he was not unlike most of the clergymen in the church.

"Well," Joe responded, " that makes you just like the rest of us. We constantly do things by the seat of our pants."

Mutually disarmed, and refreshed by a continuing give and take of candor, the two men made their way to the Rector's office, reassuring themselves that the available materials about fund raising and leadership would see them through. Not the blind leading the blind, but surely the cautious tugging at the cautious.

The first thing these men did was exchange ideas about the parish. What was the problem here? The Rector's list revealed obvious symptoms: bad repair, casualness about commitments, financial trouble, no real future that people could identify with, just boredom. The choir was terrible and the brunt of coffee-hour jokes. The sermons were less than exciting. But what was the real problem, the crucial illness? Apathy. Nobody really cared.

Joe confessed that his list would have revealed the same things. The parish might be doing a variety of things, but it meant little to Betty and him, or to the children. Now Joe was sorry he had torn up his own list, but nevertheless he was pleased to find that they were standing on the same ground.

Taking Stock

The Rector asked Joe to take part in two brief exercises he had read about which were designed to help persons discover something about themselves.[1] Joe was willing.

The first was simple enough. Each took a piece of paper and drew a horizontal line across the page, to represent a life line. They were to put a check on that part of the line where they currently felt they were in terms of age and personal growth.

After a few seconds, they exchanged papers and, to their surprise, found that each had put the check only a little past midpoint. Joe and the Rector discussed this. It was interesting to each of them that while they had all sorts of pessimistic feelings about the parish they, themselves, were optimistic about their own lives. Each felt he was not a has-been. As persons, they had plenty to do before they were through.

The Rector showed Joe the second exercise. Each took ten pieces of paper. On each sheet they were to write separate answers to the question, *Who am I*? No matter what framework they used, role, qualities, traits, physical makeup, whatever, they were to write separate answers, one per page.

When they had finished writing, they put them in rank order, placing first those which were most essentially the real person and ending with the dispensable items, those whose loss would not seriously affect the most essential qualities. Joe found this next to impossible. One quality without the other would mean that he was less of a person. This was annoying. And threatening. Why did he get involved in this dumb thing anyway?

The Rector asked that they go one step further. They were to discard the sheets of paper one at a time until all ten were discarded. After more thought, they repeated the process and ranked all ten once again. What qualities could they really live without? What was most essential after all? This was what they discussed on into the dinner hour.

The two men were embarrassed, and made jokes about the artificiality of the exercises, but agreed that it got down to some real basics about their views of themselves. They were similiar. They felt inadequate for many jobs they had to do, but were sure they could accomplish what had to be done. Joe had willingness, drive and, as it seemed, a determination to achieve.

But achieve what? Joe had no interest in wasting his time on "causes." Especially during the last days of the tennis season. Nevertheless, Joe heard himself saying, "All right, I'll be your chairman of the Every Member Canvass." The Rector smiled broadly, and Joe quickly added, "For this year only."

Membership

"Exactly what does it mean to be a member of the Episcopal Church?" Joe wanted to know. He was unsure where the chairmanship of the Every Member Canvass would lead him; but he was doubly unsure of where his lifelong church membership had brought him. He needed to find out.

The Rector suggested as a start that each take a copy of the *Constitution and Canons of the Episcopal Church* and, before Sunday, read the section on membership.[2] Such reading might be terse and cold but it was, at least, as basic as one could get. The Rector would preach on the material that Sunday, and Joe and he could compare notes the following week before the first meeting of the committee. They wondered aloud about the critics who said that, when it came to matters of basics, members of the Episcopal Church had their feet firmly planted in midair. Would the Canons bear this out?

Joe's reading revealed some remarkable items. Specifically, he had received the Sacrament of Holy Baptism with water, in the name of the Father, and of the Son, and of the Holy Spirit. This fact had been duly noted in a record book located in the parish of his youth. He had also been confirmed by a bishop of the church, and this too had been duly recorded.

Joe Joiner had said publicly that he believed, and put his truth in the fact, that Jesus Christ had released him from sin, sanctified him with the Holy Spirit, and would give him the kingdom of heaven and everlasting life. Because of this, Joe had renounced the devil and all his works, the vain pomp and glory of the world, with all covetous desires of the same, and the sinful desires of the flesh. Moreover, Joe was to recite the Apostles' Creed, that sparse statement that grounded the spiritual to the temporal, not necessarily because he had to but because this was the most succinct way he could express what it is all about.

So, in the company of millions of others whom he would never meet let alone know by name, Joe had stated that he really believed in Jesus the Christ, the son of the living God. He accepted Christ as his personal saviour, and he desired to follow Him unashamedly, and no matter what. Joe's membership in good standing was contingent on the fact that he actively recall the presence of his Lord and Saviour by receiving Holy Communion at least three times a year. That surely would not interfere with his tennis game.

Or would it? This had been a difficult weekend for Joe. The Rector's sermon on Sunday reinforced what he had read. The exercises had revealed that he wanted to be fulfilled as a human being. He had real needs to understand himself and the world around him. He really did want to believe everything the Canons said, but found it difficult. He felt he believed in God, and wanted God to be a part of his life. Or, was it the other way around? He wanted to be part of God's world. But he also wanted to play tennis on Sunday mornings.

Patterns

Although Joe Joiner had reluctantly accepted the invitation to be a leader in the parish, he wanted to be a good one. So, for the next few days he made an assessment of leadership—by reading some of the materials the Rector gave him and by thinking about all the leaders there were in the world.

What did he expect from any leader? What would people expect from his leadership?

He asked himself a series of questions. Would he know his job? Would he treat others as he would have them treat him? Would people have to get around him to get the job done? Would his personal agenda get in the way? Would they learn something of value from him? Would he learn from them? After the job was over, would they ever ask him to accept a leadership role again? Joe concluded that he wanted to get the job done, whatever it might be, and he wanted to win friends and influence others in the process of doing it. He felt sure that those working with him would want the very same things.

Who—What—was a leader? Well, he was someone who took the necessary risks to get the job done.

Did all this mean that Joe would have to be a tyrant, a despot, a dictator, a loner? They always told him that the chairman of committees did all the work. That was the natural order of things. And perhaps for good reasons. Working with others might just hamper the process. He had to choose a leadership style for himself.

If Joe made the decision himself and announced it, his committee people would have little area of freedom to act and react. This sounded safe, but not too sound. If they had little opportunity to share with his decision, they would criticize him behind his back, and maybe even sabotage his decision.

Should he tell others exactly what to do? Would he endorse whatever they wanted to do? Was there something in between? Or was there some variation on these themes? The answer lay in the degree of risk. The leader, to repeat, was one who would have the guts to take whatever risks were necessary to get the right things done.[3]

Joe went over the various patterns of leadership available to him.[4] What about the possibility of making the decisions privately, and *then* going over them with others? This could save a lot of time and fuss.

Or, what if he made the decision privately, but then invited questions from the others? This made a stab at sharing, and that might keep everyone happy. It would keep resistance to a minimum. On the positive side, it provided a chance to explore the decision, perhaps early enough to catch mistakes before they occurred. The leader, however, remained the final judge.

Then again, Joe could present not a final decision but, rather, the problem about which he would encourage discussion from others. This gave a great deal of freedom for others to give suggestions. Then the leader, selecting what he felt to be the best of the suggestions, could proceed to make his private decision.

Still, he could open up the areas of group participation more by presenting the problem, giving the dimensions limiting their decision, and then allowing the others to join him in making the final decision.

Finally, of course, he could present the problem, sit back

and allow the others to make the necessary decision. This offered the most freedom, but the least control by him.

Somewhere within those patterns Joe felt sure he would find a compromise style he could call his own. He suspected it lay somewhere between participatory democracy and dictatorship. . . .

The telephone rang. It was the Rector.

"I have a committee for you, Joe," the Rector reported. "Some newer members like yourself. Is next Monday night all right? At eight o'clock? . . . Thanks again, Joe."

So this was it. This was what? Joe wondered whether or not he would serve the church, and if the church would serve him. He looked again at the stack of reading material the Rector had given him. So this was it, eh? Was this what was meant by a calling?

B.
The Renewal Committee

INTRODUCTIONS

For a Monday night in September there was more than a usual chill in the air, Joe Joiner noted as he left his car and walked to the parish house for his first meeting with the members of the Every Member Canvass. He stubbed his toe on the path leading to the side door. Only then did he realize how inadequate the lighting was. One should not put spotlights on peeling walls or on weed-choked lawns, but nevertheless, better lighting made sense. Or was the parish hiding its light under a bushel for good reason?

Joe's thoughts turned to the parish, about which he knew very little. He would have to subscribe to the notion that he, as *leader*, strengthened with the traits, characteristics, and principles that he would try to perceive as the operation of the Holy Spirit in his life, would put into action the *proper means*, which were the play and interplay of specifics, so the *participants*, whoever they might be, would understand and respond for the purpose of accomplishing the *goal*, with the greatest effectiveness, with the minimum of confusion, and with the maximum of charity. Was this what he had learned from his reading?

Pausing for two deep breaths, Joe opened the door to the parish hall. He was met by four people in one very large room—the Rector and three parishioners. The Rector greeted him, and said five others thought they might be able to attend the meeting, but could not promise. Two more said they would be there late, and would the others please start without them. For this Joe Joiner had spent hours reading and thinking and, oh yes, giving up two doubles matches?

Joe forced a smile as his glance took in the large room and few people. "Would you mind taking a chair and forming a circle near this wall? Nothing like having an intimate conversation in the middle of the Grand Canyon, is there?"

The Rector asked that they say the Lord's Prayer in unison, and then introduced Joe Joiner, the new parishioner, an architect by vocation, who would give some artistic scope and form to their current needs—or words to that effect. Joe volleyed by telling them that he usually worked alone and only met with others when he had finished blueprints to submit. He could tell by their faces that this admission of being a loner, and an artistic one at that, did not go over well.

He asked each person to introduce himself. Vic Verve was the first: a lifelong member here, and glad they were finally getting the show on the road. Skip Skeptic spoke next. He was always glad that plans would be made for churches of all kinds, this one included, but doubted that anything good would come of it. Third was Angie Angry. She had not laughed at Joe's Grand Canyon joke. She refused to speak at this time, preferring to reserve comment until she had more facts. She continued with her knitting.

So this was his Every Member Canvass committee. So this was the parish. Was this the Episcopal Church? Yes, Joe guessed it was. Its members were the likes of Joe, and the rest of them here on a chilly Monday night. Okay. He would start where he was.

Joe thanked them for coming, and explained that he did not know much about the parish really, or the Episcopal Church for that matter, but had accepted this job as chairman anyway. He had read somewhere that people usually give money for great causes rather than to needy institutions,[5] and he would use this as his theme song. He was not sure he was the right man for this job, but his wife, Betty, thought he was. So did the Rector. He paused, hoping for some response, but none came. He went on, therefore, to tell them that if he did anything he would have them change the name of the committee to something that sounded better. The name Every Member Canvass sounded to him more like a judo lesson to be held in some gym. Vic Verve laughed at that one, but Skip Skeptic and the Rector just coughed. Angie Angry looked at her watch. An impossible situation, Joe thought as he talked.

Just then in walked smiling Pauline Politic, who held the door open for obviously cheerful Patricia—would you please call her Pat—Pious. They had attended Pat's second gathering of a prayer group earlier in the evening, but, as Pauline said, they would not have missed this meeting for the world. "Have we missed anything?" she asked.

Joe had three items on his mind. First, that he and the Rector had agreed that things were not going as well as they could here at the parish. Second, that a larger committee would have to meet next Saturday morning. Third, that the Rector had come across a recent study which might give them food for thought, if not a bit of optimism, as they attempted to make things work here. No one seemed to like the idea of meeting Saturday morning, and Joe was sorry he had brought it up at this time. He quickly jumped to the third point, the study.

Studies

A couple of years ago, Joe told them, an in-depth study had been made of 367 Episcopal parishes in the United States to discover why their communicant giving was so much higher than the average for other Episcopal parishes.[6]

The conclusions would be important to them. Selected key people right within a parish made it a success, no matter how much outside help they received. If there were not enough local, dedicated people who were willing to make it a personal effort with full use of visitations, sermons, and teaching, there was no sense starting.

The style used most successfully by these parishes was a low-key emphasis of Christian commitment, via the teaching of the faith. The people wanted to know what was going on, and what was planned for the future. They wanted assurance that the leadership cared for them personally, and wanted their personal support. They wanted candor and clarity. They did *not* want to be hit with sledgehammer-type threats.

The result of these efforts, the study went on to reveal, was a better parish. Increasing financial support had had no adverse effect on the congregation. Just the opposite was true. The parishioners were talking about spiritual awakening, tithing, knowing more about the faith and practice of the church. They had become enthusiastic and knowledgeable members.

"So much pie in the sky," remarked Skip Skeptic as he cracked his knuckles. "But," he added, "miracles can happen, even here."

Pauline knew the Rector and Joe would do whatever was necessary, and she felt it was her duty to assist them in every way. She would not offer any suggestions about method at this time; whatever the Rector wanted was all right with her. Angie looked from her watch to the high heavens with that comment. No, she had no comment of her own to make. Pat Pious wanted to speak, but Vic Verve jumped to his feet. In six or seven breathless sentences, Vic outlined a procedure whereby each of them could telephone forty members before Sunday and ask them all to increase their pledges by fifty percent. As a matter of fact, *he* would start making his calls that evening when he got home.

Joe seized his opportunity to use Vic's enthusiasm. He thanked him for the spirit of optimism, but asked if they would consider his second point of the evening first. It was necessary to gather a larger committee, and to deal with the specific issues of this parish in detail. To meet Saturday morning was his suggestion. He would give up a tennis match, and he could play in the afternoon. He'd be more alert for a morning meeting. Would this be all right? Would they attend?

They agreed to meet, with the hope, expressed by Skip, that someone might come up with an agenda. Joe hoped he would have one. He also hoped that the Rector would invite the Vestry and the members of the Finance Committee to join them. The Rector said he would do his best. Joe then asked each of them to do some homework. Would they kindly list on paper what they felt were the *good* things and the *bad* things about the parish. Angie said she could write a book on the bad things alone. Joe hoped she wouldn't just yet, it might discourage them all. Pauline smiled. Angie, stony faced, looked at her watch.

Pat Pious had a request. "May I bring a few members of the prayer group to the meeting on Saturday?

"Is this really their concern?" asked Skip. "I mean, we're going to be talking about money and budgets and things like that. I doubt even your group could pray us out of the mess we're in."

"You never can tell," answered Pat with a smile. "You never can tell."

Joe thought they were getting to sound corny so he jumped in and said something about not wanting a theological discussion right now, and that the more the merrier was the key so Pat should bring all the people she wanted. Joe thought to himself that he wanted quantity of participation. The quality, he hoped, would come later.

And then Joe thanked them and said the meeting was over. Pauline, with a gentle reprimand, asked if the Rector would dismiss them with his blessing, and Joe, too embarrassed to speak, gestured to the Rector. The Rector blessed them, and they all went home.

Assessment

During the few days preceding the next meeting of the committee, Joe tried hard to analyze the events of Monday night.

Did that gathering represent the best that the parish had to offer? He guessed so. Some of them would never be at any meeting he was involved in at his firm in town, but he could not judge them on that basis. This was not a commercial business even though running a parish was similar in some ways to running a business. At least, at this point, he thought so. So did Skip Skeptic. Yes, these few people were perhaps as typical as he was to expect. These were the people he would have to deal with.

Pat Pious puzzled him, though. He knew she had a place in all this, of course, but where he was not sure. The Rector had been supportive by allowing Joe to chair the meeting fully. That was important. Joe, after all, was the person the committee had to deal with. He had pushed his own agenda, inept as it was, because he felt he had to take control in a shakedown-type cruise, as Monday night surely was. But if he had given any impression of despotic behavior they would be waiting for him next time, hiding in coves with cannons loaded and pointed right between his eyes. He would have to watch for that.

Meetings

Why did so many people hate to attend meetings? And, interestingly enough, why did those who attended the most meetings like them the least, even though they would not miss them for the world? Joe thought about this as he probed into the materials on leadership.

Meetings were where things happened between people. Meetings were where unrelated people related, either by tugging with or against each other. Meetings were where people came to grips with themselves if not others. It was where change could take place, where growth could have a chance. Meetings were the focal point in society. They were a mixture of wasted and renewed time and talent.

Meetings would be a fact of Joe's life during these next months. How would he share power? How would he reconcile the superior/subordinate relationships as they occurred? Using a guide, which talked about the differences between "judgmental and judicious" management,[7] he asked himself the following questions:

Was it best to have one boss call all the shots? Or, was it better to use cooperatively the various talents available to him?

Must Joe protect his power to make decisions? Or, would the best decision emerge if he combined his power with that of those who would eventually have to implement them?

Did Joe have to decide every course of action where he had authority to decide? Or should he enlist his subordinates to devise courses of action, and then contribute his own thoughts as matters progressed?

Must Joe exercise all the autonomy his power permitted? Or should he use his power to help each subordinate develop his or her autonomy?

Should Joe use his power for his own growth? Or should he share his power so that the subordinates could grow as he grew?

Should Joe motivate the group? Or should the group's accomplishments motivate the group? Could Joe provide the necessary opportunities for this accomplishment?

Must Joe review, oversee, and control the efforts of his subordinates? Or should he use his experience, power, and skill to aid subordinates in accomplishing the task?

Should Joe take credit for the results of the group? Or should he clearly recognize the accomplishments of subordinates?

To get results, must Joe spot all flaws and have them corrected? Or, to get results, should Joe help others spot and overcome any flaws?

Joe put down the article he was reading and paced the floor. Putting those ideas into action was no easy task. He grabbed two cookies, swallowed some coffee, and returned to the questions posed by the article:

When subordinates said or did things that Joe found unacceptable, should he point out the flaws? Or should he assume that they were making sense, and that he should explore the problem from that point of view?

Would Joe kid himself and say that he could take putdowns and harsh criticism without destructive consequences? Or would he admit that even the most mature persons are distressed by criticisms, and that this made cooperation difficult?

Was Joe's role to define the mission of the group? Or was his role in mission definition to facilitate discovery by the subordinates and himself?

Should Joe make judgments about the actions of his subordinates while they were carrying out the decisions? Or was Joe's role to join the subordinates, to make sure they succeeded?

That was quite a barrage of questions, and Joe was exhausted.

To be judicious meant exhibiting sound judgment. By moving so deftly from the judgmental to the judicious style, the presider, such as Joe Joiner, could free himself and the others so he could offer all his skill, experience, and knowledge without relegating the so-called subordinates to inferior positions. And if he did that correctly, he would not have to give up his duty to guide and, if need be, to control.[8] A neat trick if he could do it.

Yes, Joe was beginning to learn that to preside at meetings was more than banging a gavel on the podium or on the head of Angie Angry. But he was still tempted to do both. Leadership training took time.

TEAM DEVELOPMENT

On Saturday morning Joe and the Rector arrived a half hour early. They wanted to make sure there were enough chairs, and that they were formed in a circle near one side of the large hall. To put the chairs in rows would mean that some people would see only the backs of others, and that Joe, as presider, would loom large as the despot after all. Joe and the Rector would take chairs in the circle, along with everyone else.

Joe rehearsed the essentials of team development which,

according to one theory, demanded the balance of two external demands with three internal demands.[9]

The two external demands: *"Organization expectations* about team performance, which may be expressed in terms of production standards, acceptable levels of quality, broad policies and procedures, etc. *Relations with other groups,* which can be critical in at least three general cases: (*a*) where two or more teams work simultaneously on subsystems of some project or product which must be integrated when (*b*) two or more teams perform sequential steps on some project or product so that the work pace and quality of one team is either dependent upon and/or directly influences another team or teams where (*c*) two or more teams are related."[10]

The three internal demands: *"The group task,* whose short-run demands may be so compelling as to be overwhelming. *Group maintenance,* which refers to the management of what team members do to and with each other as they work on the common task. *Individual needs* of team members which variously influence and relate to how a team does its work, and whose relative satisfaction crucially determines the individual's involvement and commitment to his team."[11]

Joe and the Rector had started to discuss the difference between those who plan, those who make the decisions, and those who carry them out, but were interrupted by the arrival of the other members of the parish who had accepted the invitation to attend this meeting.

All those who had met with Joe the previous Monday were there. Even Skip Skeptic and Angie Angry. Plus five members of the Vestry, including the wardens, two members of the Finance Committee and, sure enough, all four members of Pat Pious's prayer group. Joe was pleased, and genuinely grateful. The Rector reinforced this by whispering to Joe that the turnout was a credit to him, and that he wished Joe the best.

ONE VIEW FROM THE PEW   27

The Rector had made sure coffee was perking and the table had enough cups and utensils, plus two trays of rolls and pastry. As the eighteen of them mingled by the refreshment table, Joe introduced himself to each person individually. He knew very few of them. They seemed to be a congenial group, and eager enough to get going, so he asked them to take seats and bring their coffee with them.

Joe had everyone introduce themselves. He had learned years ago that in the art of introductions it was best to let the person do it himself. This way everyone would get the right pronunciation if nothing else, and also it would prevent that terrible embarrassment when the oldest member's name was forgotten, or even unknown to someone who might have been sitting next to him in the same pew for years.

The introductions completed, the Rector mentioned that Joe had consented to chair this committee, which he hoped would get off the ground this morning, admitting that they were six months late in starting an Every Member Canvass.

The Rector suddenly opened a large cardboard box he had brought in earlier that morning. Joe was annoyed that he, as chairman, was not in on this surprise. The box contained numerous bulletins, parish newsletters, photographs of parish life through the years. The Rector passed these to the group and asked that they be studied, but please, no coffee spills on them. The people were puzzled and a few of them did not hide frowns and coughs. The Rector then told them that these mementos represented a glimpse of the history of their parish. He said that it represented what people were planning, thinking, and doing through the years.

During the few minutes when everyone looked at glimpses of things there were a few good-natured snickers. The older participants laughed as they recalled incidents from the past. In general, it was a good ice-breaker, and it had a point. It served to illustrate that this was what the parish thought of itself, and what it said and showed of itself. Joe, along with the newer members, was glad to get this brief, colorful indoctrination.

The Rector then turned the meeting over to Joe. Some wanted to talk about the mementos right then, but Joe asked them to hold their comments for a minute. He counted off one to four around the circle and asked the groups to take their chairs with them to each of the four corners of the hall, the "ones" meeting here, the "twos" meeting there, and so forth.

They were to spend twenty minutes discussing two questions. The first was: "What prevents life in this parish from being more satisfying?" The second was: "What would make life in this parish more rewarding for me?"[12] Joe wanted quantity of responses, so he cautioned them not to argue on one or two points, but to list everything that was said, no matter how insignificant it might seem. The four groups of four people each went to their corners. Joe and the Rector picked up the mementos left behind.

Twenty minutes later, Joe asked everyone to reassemble in the circle, so they could share the comments with one another. The recorder for each group spoke. Each of them felt that more time was needed for such an exchange of ideas. A few within the groups did not make any comments. Joe noticed, also, that one group picked the wrong convener, Curt Conflict, because it seems he was the only one in his group who spoke for the twenty minutes. Nevertheless, they did share a number of ideas.

If only Joe had remembered to supply a blackboard, it would have made it easier for them to keep the ideas in focus. Joe promised that he would correct this error before the next meeting. Furthermore, he would try to list, by categories, what this group felt were the salient points.

Joe moved on to another item, the matter of volunteers. He

believed four committees were necessary for this campaign, and would they volunteer to serve on these committees. Mentioning committees at this time was another mistake.

Vic Verve jumped to his feet. "Hey, that's great, let's get these committees going by tomorrow."

The Senior Warden was more cautious. "Don't you think it might be wise," he said, "if we were to get a better picture of who and what we are before we organized ourselves into committees?"

Joe knew down deep that the warden was right about that, but Joe felt pressed for time. He pressed forward, nevertheless, and named four committees on the grounds that he had given this much thought, and decided this was the right way to go. The warden sat back and made mental notes. Joe had lost him for the moment, hopefully not for good. Joe announced his four committees anyway.[13]

The first, the *Proposal Committee*, would create the case for the parish. It would tell what the parish wanted to do, or at least what it ought to be doing in light of its commitment to God in culture. This committee would not write the budget for the new year, but its membership, including those dealing in parish finances, would make sure realistic guidelines were maintained. Vic Verve volunteered to be the chairman.

The second was the *Communications Committee*. Its purpose was to ensure that everyone in the parish was fully aware that there really was a parish and an Every Member Canvass, and that it was to mean something of value. This committee would create, then distribute the necessary materials. Its membership would have to include those who knew media. Curt Conflict volunteered to be chairman.

The third was the *Special Events Committee*. If there was to be a dedication service, a luncheon for canvassers and a kick-off parish dinner, or anything else they might think of, this was the group to plan it and get it off the ground. Its members would be cooks, bottlewashers and hostesses, but also those who would work well with the other committee members. Pat Pious volunteered to be chairman.

The fourth was the *Contact Committee*. Its purpose was to touch base with everyone who had even the slightest relationship to the parish. It would have the largest number of members, especially if the intention was to make personal visits. Pauline Politic volunteered to be chairman.

Joe asked for volunteers to serve on these committees. He hoped they would be dedicated to the task, would have enough time to give all that was necessary, would be able to get along with the others, believed in the parish, thought the Episcopal Church was here to stay, believed things could always get better, would not lock themselves into patterns of the past, would not affect change for the sake of change only, and, of course, would rush into some phonebooth, yell *shazam*, and come out as superhumans, ready and able to jump the tallest buildings if not the bulkiest of bureaucratic pilings. They merely had to be superhuman.

Regarding their timetable, Joe told them that this was the first of a six-week schedule, so they were already on their way. He personally would make a summary of their verbal picture of the parish and send it to them, along with the names of committee members, before the beginning of next week. He would also send them what he felt to be a reasonable calendar before next week. Joe would do his own homework, but was Joe doing too much of it himself?

Then Joe asked if there were any questions. Vic wanted to know, in view of all the things Joe was to do before next week, if he, in fact, had already been successful in yelling *shazam*. Was this a mild slap? It sounded like it, especially when Angie Angry followed with, "I guess you don't need us anyway."

Had Joe made another mistake? Had he really given them the impression that he had everything thought out in detail, and therefore did not need them? This was not what he wanted them to think, at all. And it was not true.

It was getting late; he thanked them for attending, and said that he would entertain a motion of adjournment.

Pat Pious rose to her feet. She had a question. "Is the purpose of this canvass to raise money or to lower the depths of spirituality?" The meeting was not to end so soon.

Renewal

This question extended the meeting for forty-five minutes, as they bantered comments around, such as: You can't worry about religious things until you fix the leaky ceiling . . . We can't do everything at once so let's get the money first . . . It's our responsibility to write a budget and sell that and that alone . . . Writing a letter, as a matter of fact, is all we have time for; it's silly to think otherwise . . . If we push them too hard on all this fancy talk we're just going to confuse the issue by giving them too much to think of . . . To sustain this thing for six weeks is impossible . . . It's embarrassing to think we can talk to others about the faith . . . The parish has to be run as a business; let's keep the religious stuff out of it . . . Right, the Rector can do that in church, and we'll hit them with the pledge card during the week. . . . Joe felt he had lost control of the meeting, and comments were coming pell-mell.

The Rector asked for the floor. He wanted to read a few paragraphs which had meant much to him. They had to do with *Stewardship*, that often used but little understood concept in the church. Would they please consider the following?

> Stewardship is a piece of that complex puzzle called the Church. Stewardship is a piece of that complex life called you. Proper stewardship is a thankful response for a life being put together by God's love. Stewardship is reality. God is real and you can be too.[14]

Would they also consider:

> The Theology of Stewardship is the systematic attempt of Christian thought to clarify the significance of that divine activity for the life of man, and to guide intelligently the response which it calls forth.[15]

Curt Conflict wanted the floor. He had been silent during much of this discussion but now felt it was time to remind the Rector that the problem with the church was that the clergy were very good at pious phrases and generalizations but left much to be desired when it got to specifics. "For instance," he continued, "I read where all rectors were good on the offertory, but not much at passing the plate."[16]

Joe was embarrassed for the Rector and he was also confused. "Curt," Joe asked, "I don't get it."

Curt took his time answering. "If you thought about it, you'd realize that talk is cheap. The pious phrases are one thing, but rolling up the sleeves and getting out there where the pocketbooks are is something else."

There was silence except for a "Hear, hear!" from Angie. It looked to Joe that Curt wanted to pick a fight, but he thought that a fight at this time would be counter-productive. Joe eased them out of this by thanking Curt for this important reminder, which really applied to each of them, not just the clergy. It would be mandatory to speak in specifics as they attempted to sell their case to the parishioners. It would of necessity be a person-to-person witness of a very personal commitment to what the church stood for.

"Whatever those fancy words mean," said Curt Conflict, sarcastically.

The Senior Warden responded, "And that's what we'll try to find out, won't we?"

Joe was determined to end this meeting on a positive note, and he tried to build from Curt's obvious anger. "Look," he said, "Curt has helped me with something that has been bugging me all along. The title of this effort should be something more meaningful than Every Member Canvass. Do you agree?"

Not too many agreed that the name should be changed. Some were tired and didn't appreciate late-hour attempts at reconciliation. It was an acceptable title, so why not keep it. Moreover, if it worked well in the past, why shouldn't it work now? The arguments continued. Then came two suggestions for "stewardship" as the name, since that's what it was anyway. Pat Pious wanted the floor. Joe didn't want to give it to her. In his mind, she was the problem of the evening, getting people to argue just when the meeting should have ended. But she got the floor, nevertheless.

"Would you consider," Pat asked, "calling this "Our Renewal Committee." It seemed to her that the parish was attempting to come alive in the spirit, and that was what renewal was all about. "This title," she concluded, "is far from unique, but it does capture the feeling of the meeting." And, looking straight at Joe, "Don't you agree?"

Joe, in turn, asked the group if they agreed with this suggestion. He was not going to let her pin him to the wall. There was some arguing about dropping the "Our," and then replacing the "Our" with "Your" to make it more personal, and after another ten minutes, they finally agreed upon *Renewal Committee*. Just two words.

Joe said that it was very late, and he was grateful that they were willing to spend so much time, and, if they were willing to continue this same commitment of time and talent during the weeks ahead, they could not fail.

"As long," jabbed Skip Skeptic, "as Pat's ladies can conjure up meetings that are better organized."

"That will be the day," added Angie Angry.

"Relax, Angie, Skip, and the rest of you. Relax, will you!" Joe was tired and did all he could to refrain from telling them where they could go. He forced a smile, nevertheless, and made some feeble joke about having to serve breakfast if they did not end this meeting, so, if the Rector would be kind enough to dismiss them with his blessing, they would call the meeting adjourned.

Skip Skeptic and Angie Angry did not say goodnight to anyone when they left the meeting.

Joe went home tired but, in some ways which he could not discern fully, pleased. Right or wrong, good or bad, he was at least doing something.

C.
Assessment and Renewal

Joe Joiner thought some more about the process so far: the meetings themselves, and a task he had asked the Vestry to perform. First, the meetings.

He wanted to avoid dominating the group, but his insecurities forced him into taking over. The more insecure he felt, the more domineering he became. He would have to watch that. He surely tried to let everyone express themselves, even to the point of allowing the angry ones to speak their piece. But did he really? He still preferred not to have the angry ones ruin things, but he knew they had to get their anger out into the open if this group was to move ahead. He tried not to answer all the questions himself, but, rather, open it for general discussion. But at least one person, Curt, had accused him of stacking the deck. Most important, perhaps, was his readiness to build positively on what was said. Perhaps it was not so bad as it could have been. Yes, maybe he was learning something after all.

Joe was learning more about meetings. He could not succeed if he arrived at the meetings filled to the brim with conclusions.

He needed to call for information, to put all kinds of comments into verbal play, so the group itself could discover the conclusions. Direction was the need in subsequent meetings, and flexibility was the style. Above all, meetings were group activities where groups made decisions.[17]

Corrections

Joe made an informal checklist of things to remember for the future.

1. *Mechanics*: Have newsprint and marking pencils, or a blackboard so everyone could share in the same information simultaneously. Have a staff person available to keep the minutes and other remarks. Furthermore, if there was to be an agenda, which there surely should be, it should be spelled out at the start of the meeting, so everyone was sure where the meeting was going, what its dimensions would be, including its procedural style in general. Furthermore, they would not take each other by surprise, as the Rector had done with his so-called box of historical material. It was a good and necessary "launching-device,"[18] something to get people talking and thinking about the same issue, but it should have been worked out beforehand. Moreover, the "stewardship" discussion would have been more effective had it been planned beforehand.

2. *Key people*: If at all possible, he would attempt to brief the conveners of any buzz groups beforehand. He would also try to select the chairmen of the various committees, ascertain their willingness to accept the call beforehand, and announce the selection at the meeting. And he should appoint a recorder for each group. This planning would give Joe the chance to get the best possible combinations of parishioner, doing the

right jobs, without allowing for embarrassing on-the-spot assessments of their qualifications, or adverse reactions from the others.

3. *Getting the right things accomplished*: For what reason were these people meeting? To agree on what chalk to use on the blackboard? To draw lots to see who would bring the coffee and cake next time? To make an in-depth study of whether the final report of the committee should be written with a black rather than blue ballpoint pen? Joe suspected that many a church committee exhausted itself on blue versus black ink. Well, this committee would have to focus on more important issues, such as the survival of the parish and the mission of the church in contemporary society.

Function

How did one go about finding the mission of the local parish? By finding out, first of all, where the parish was at the present time. The Renewal Committee would study the answers to the question "What makes the parish?" and it would also take a close look at something being done by the Vestry. Joe had asked the Senior Warden to have the Vestry fill in a "Parish Profile."[19]

Under fourteen separate headings the Vestry would make every effort to discover who and what the parish really was: (1) The neighborhood setting. (2) The location of the parish membership. (3) Description of the parish properties. (4) Membership statistics. (5) History of clergy and lay readers over the past twenty years. (6) The present leadership. (7) Worship patterns and statistics. (8) Christian evangelism and visitation. (9) Communications. (10) Christian education.

(11) Church school. (12) Community and neighborhood outreach. (13) Participation in diocesan and national church programs. (14) Finances. When the results of this survey were in Joe's hands, he would have a comprehensive picture of the situation.

Now Joe was beginning to understand the Senior Warden's earlier question: "Don't you think it might be wise if we were to get a better picture of who and what we are before we organize ourselves into committees?" Or, to put it another way, in all organizations it is wise to have *function precede form; that is, decide what you want to do before organizing yourself to do it.*

Joe imagined that too often organizations built sturdy office space, and hired sturdier individuals, and laid out the most intricate organizational charts and retirement programs *before* deciding what the organization really wanted to do. No wonder these organizations fell flat.

And then Joe laughed to himself. Was the Rector more clever than Joe first suspected? Did the Rector, in concert with other parishioners, conclude that what the parish needed was to develop new talent from among the parishioners whose motivation never got beyond the back pew? How tricky!

Okay. Back to the point about function and form. What was the parish trying to do? What was its business? Once discovered, then the parish could organize itself to do exactly what it needed to do. Its form would be determined by its function.

It was getting late. Neither Betty nor the boys had seen him all day. Had he learned anything of value? Joe went over some notes from his reading. He had two brief summaries about meetings and planning. These he would remember and, he hoped, make part of his conduct from here on.

Concerning meetings: Joe rehearsed the three essential points for all meetings. There was a need to accomplish the *goal* whatever it might eventually be. Second, there was a need to maintain the *integrity of the group* itself. And third, there was a need to guarantee that, somehow, the individual would sense a genuine feeling of purpose and *participation*.[20]

Concerning planning: Joe reviewed some basics about the rationale for planning. There were three points to remember: (1) to provide a *comprehensive* framework so, when decision making took place, one element could relate to all others and the whole; (2) to provide a *disciplined* framework so, in the process of decision making, all those taking part would be working within the same boundaries and priorities; (3) to provide a *projective* framework so, in the process of decision making, those participating would be related to the realistic methods and mechanics of current action.[21]

Well, Joe Joiner as leader got through his first week with the Renewal Committee. Only five more to go. Five what? Five "minutes," because he would never have enough time; five "years," because the pressures would go on endlessly. A little of both, he concluded. He would have to learn how to master the most common ingredient of a leader's world: time. Would Joe have time?

IT'S ABOUT TIME

Joe Joiner, as leader, had unique skills and, lest he forget, unique failings, but there was one thing he shared with everyone else in creation. It was *time*. He consumed time ravenously, continuously. He sliced it into pieces, he chewed it up, he gulped it down, and he always came back for more.

He could not buy this delicacy, time. The supply was plentiful, but exhaustible. He could not lock it in the cupboard, or make it expand in the oven. He could not wrap it in foil for another day, he could not freeze it for next week's meeting. It was here, always to be consumed. It was here, then gone forever, and there was nothing to take its place.

To sum up, Joe's life as a leader began, continued, and ended not in fancy schemes but in time. What would distinguish him as a leader would be his "tender loving care of time."[22]

But how? How could he cultivate a tender loving care of time? Joe had his business to attend to, his family, his commuting, his relaxation in front of the television set, his eating, grooming, and sleeping. And his tennis game, which he was missing more and more.

Chairing the Renewal Committee meant meetings, conversations, memos, documents, readings, all kinds of details. He was being pulled in a hundred directions at once. Could he do all that was necessary, in the allotted time, and still keep his sanity?

Joe thought he'd better relax or he'd start imagining things. For instance, the wristwatch he was looking at as he walked from one end of his den to the other was not an enemy, it was small, round, gold-filled, and easy on the eyes. It had a sweep second hand which he swore was moving faster and faster as he thought about this, but that was silly. The watch was in good repair. The calendar flipped the day of the week and the date of the month with stunning precision and accuracy. This watch was not an enemy, but a friend. He had to treat it as such. It was not a monster. It was inanimate. He had to deal with it, he had to control it and not let it control him. He had to discover how to manage his time. But how?

Necessities

Joe studied a list of those items that took so much of his time. Commuting, waiting for others, visitors, unexpected interruptions, mediocre assistance, lack of preparation, failure to delegate, misplaced items, reading irrelevant material, unnecessary correspondence, long letters, telephone interruptions, coffee breaks, procrastination, routine details, and just plain poor organization.[23]

There were a myriad of time wasters in any organization. Joe's pet peeve was the late arriver. There was nothing more disconcerting for a chairman of a meeting to be interrupted by the tardiness of anyone, no matter how popular or important that person might be. He remembered losing his equanimity the time Pat Pious and Pauline Politic arrived late to his first meeting. He would lose his temper and burn quietly whenever another chairman would stop in the middle of a sentence to recognize the late arriver, or worse, stop the proceedings to go over the items of business for the benefit of the indolent. Joe's approach would be to ignore the latecomer and move right along. His justification for doing this would be twofold: reduce attention to the indolent that the indolent seemed to want in the first place, and not punish those who were willing to get there on time. Of course, certain circumstances would alter this procedure, but basically it would be his code of conduct.

Joe remembered an incident with his wife, Betty, before they were married. They had known each other for many years, had grown up in the same town, and had, over the years, taken each other for granted. They were not sure of each other and they wondered whether or not they should break their engagement. Their uncertainty led to subtle warfare.

Whenever they made a date, it was inevitable that one or the other would be late. Cooling the heels became a pattern, first with Joe, and then with Betty. It got so that the one who arrived late was the winner of the battle. The one who arrived late forced the attention on him or her. It was a struggle for power.

Would this same struggle for power come into play at meetings? Joe supposed it would, and he would have to look out for it. He would also have to make sure that he never resorted to lateness in starting any meeting, for exactly the same reasons.

But back to the matter of time.

Those who wasted time were a subtle lot. Joe recognized four concerns in this matter.[24] First, he must beware the *recurring crisis*. One crisis was to be expected; to have it pop up again and again was a fatal error. He would have to make every effort to spot its possibility beforehand, thereby affecting the changes that would eliminate or minimize it.

Second, he must avoid the destruction of time through *overstaffing*. Don't discourage volunteers, but keep the organization as lean as possible, nevertheless. It would make an easier climb up those bureaucratic hills.

Third, avoid *excess meetings*. It was true that meetings were vital to the life of any organization, but he was reminded that they were "a concession to deficient organization. For one either meets or works. One cannot do both at the same time."[25] The clearer everyone was about his or her role within the parish, the less need there was to have meetings every time one turned around.

Fourth, be alert to a *malfunctioning organization*, either in its construction or its distribution. He must make sure every key person received all necessary information, and in a manner that was understandable at first glance.[26]

These guides would be helpful to Joe, not only for the sake

of making the Renewal Committee work more efficiently, but, of course, to keep Joe's personal time schedule in check.

In the course of Joe's day, there were many things that he had to attend to. That went without saying. But was each of them equally vital to him? Was selecting a tie in the same category as, let's say, selecting a specialist to treat his son's ear infection? Was going to bed fifteen minutes later than usual as crucial as being fifteen minutes late for a meeting with his boss? Of course not. Was reading third-class mail really the same as reading a letter addressed directly to him? It shouldn't be. He had to deal with all these items in the course of the day, but some were more important than others. The test of wisdom would be to learn how to distinguish between the important and the less important, and the faster he could see the difference, the more effective a leader he would be.

To use time wisely meant to use his people wisely. And that meant managing himself. Okay, it was about time he got back to the Renewal Committee.

THE DAYS GROW SHORT

Working with others took more time than doing it yourself, but it was the only way to get more things done. Joe reminded himself of this more than once during the remaining five weeks[27] when the Renewal Committee went through its paces, from preparation to zero hour when all the parishioners would be met, head-on.

Fifth Week

Joe had four tasks to accomplish. The committee chairmen and he would have to summarize the data they had collected about the parish and put them into workable information for the proposal. They would also have to bring the parish list up to date to know exactly what their potential was. Moreover, they would have to decide on a week-to-week calendar and have it reproduced for every key person. And finally, they would all have to agree as to exactly what they were trying to do.

Framework

Thanks to the agonies of another committee from another diocese, they had, for discussion purposes, a framework for looking at a parish. (See Table 1.)[28]

The committee chairmen, Vic Verve (Proposal), Curt Conflict (Communications), Pat Pious (Special Events), and Pauline Politic (Contact) were a surprisingly congenial group now that they had something concrete to discuss. They thought the "framework" was too general, even vague, but agreed that it was an excellent skeleton upon which they could build with specific programming.

Joe, not unlike the others, knew that the words spoke of something vital to his life but, as yet, he did not understand what it was. He had not agonized through the process to develop the framework. It was good, but still not his, personally.

They discussed other salient facts and impressions.

The research by the Rector and the part-time secretary,

Table 1
A FRAMEWORK FOR LOOKING AT A PARISH

Identity—"Two or More Persons Gathered Together . . ."

Connectedness	A parish has some basis or symbol that unites it and sets it apart from other communities. In ways suited to its own life it has a
Stability	defined management pattern, traditions which form a constructive stability and
Responsibility	visibly responsible representatives with defined and active relationships with its own people, the local community, and the Diocesan family.

Commitment—"Intention and a Developed Means of Implementation"

Purposes	Each parish organization specifies its reason for being in its long- and short-range objectives, in the pursuit of which
Plan	it develops a program plan with well-defined tasks including a realistic and effective financial plan
Resources	supported by members' commitment of personal resources of talents and money, balanced between maintenance of necessary physical plant and direct involvement with people in proportions which are consistent with the parish objectives.

Works—"Outward and Visible Sign . . ."

Worship	The parish provides the scene for corporate witness through liturgical worship and recognizes
Education	education and growth as an ongoing commitment for Christians of all ages, and
Fellowship	it provides occasions for celebration of the community, to realize the joyful experience of the new life which we can carry out into
Evangelism	relationships with all people both within and outside the parish.

revealed two hundred members of the parish, some more active than others. Normally they counted on continuous support from half that number. Twenty percent of the members accounted for eighty percent of the total money received.

The town had some light industry, but only thirty-five percent of the town's population worked locally. The remainder commuted. There was one pocket of wealthy people, and a few of them attended the parish. Most of the parishioners, however, were middle to lower-middle class, owning or renting homes.

Property and school taxes had risen sharply in the last decade, which put an ever increasing burden on everyone, particularly the younger families and the elderly. As a matter of fact, many of the retired families had to sell their homes, which they could no longer afford to maintain, and were moving into retirement settlements, usually out of the community.

At the turn of the century, a section was established for the blacks, and that had not changed much except for occasional blacks who moved into other sections of the town. The black community, along with other minorities, accounted for a little less than ten percent of the population.

Public transportation was poor, and most of the residents struggled to keep one or two cars. School budgets, highway improvements, wages of county employees, and the conflicting reports on whether or not the town really needed the extension on the village hall were the issues uppermost in people's minds for the last few years. Everyone was making more money than ever before, but it was increasingly more difficult to save any of it. The discretionary dollar was disappearing fast. Money was always the topic, no matter if the conversation started with the weather (which somehow got around to air conditioning for the bedroom if not the school auditorium) or with the price of meat (which usually started with some older person reminding everyone about how much a leg of lamb used to cost). It was money. It was always money.

If money was the headache, being asked to put more and more of it in the alms basin was not the sedative. Fund raising was a pain. To avoid church might be a way of avoiding any commitments; then no one would have their feelings hurt.

Pat Pious asked a question. "Does this have any bearing on what we said was the greatest malaise of the church, namely, apathy?"

"Neat point," Vic Verve retorted. "A lack of deep feelings for the parish might just be another way of forcing yourself to avoid the issue of commitment."

"A psychological copout," concluded Curt Conflict.

Joe asked them to consider the thought that, if they did indeed represent the feeling of the majority of their parish, they had a great deal of educating to do before they could expect financial donations of any realistic kind. "We need a case," Joe said. "We need a statement about who and what we are and why. We need the very committees I formed last week."

"Yes," said the Senior Warden," the very forms which, unfortunately, preceded the disclosure of function. We did say that function preceded form, didn't we?" Joe smiled and said he stood corrected.

Joe asked if he was correct in suggesting that the Renewal Committee had two major *objectives*. (Joe told them he was using the word "objective" to signify an overall goal, as distinguished from a specific task; as the military would use *strategy* over against *tactics*.)

The first objective of the Renewal Committee was to sell the idea of the parish and what it stood for, and how it related to the Episcopal Church in general. The second objective was to create and maintain standards for financial support not only for this year's campaign but for an extended period of time.

The chairmen agreed to these objectives, reminding themselves once again that they were talking about commitments of time and talent as well as hard cash.

So far they had their objectives. They had a current list of parishioners. They had some idea of the community and the potential. They had a feeling for the general attitudes about

Table 2

PARISH RENEWAL COMMITTEE CALENDAR
(Fourth Quarter Campaign)

Week	Sunday	Monday	Tuesday	Wednesday	Thursday	Friday	Saturday
		THE FIRST THREE WEEKS OF ORGANIZATION, PREPARATION					
	Nature of Church Membership Explained	Chairman Selected by Rector and Warden				Leadership Group Meets	Larger Group Meets
	Initial Announcement Made	Initial Request for Volunteers					
	Theology of Stewardship Expressed	Proposal Finalized and Mailed to Parishioners				Draft for Proposal Discussed	
						Initial Gifts and Other Commitments	Callers Trained

THE ONE WEEK FOR PRESENTATION, SOLICITATION

| Presentation of Proposal to Parish w/Initial Gifts | Contact Procedures Launched | Cabinet Meets for Assessment | Contacts Finished |

THE FINAL TWO WEEKS OF FOLLOW THROUGH, RECOMMENDATIONS

| Results Given to Parishioners | Last Efforts to Secure Commitments | Adjustments to Proposal and Budget | |
| Revised Program Explained | Thank-Yous to Parish Sent | Full Committee Meets for Dinner Meeting Assessment | Cabinet Offers Recommendations for Next Year |

Recommendation will include anything that will be of help to the leaders as they look to the next year.

what they were up against. Now they considered the timetable and calendar.

Using the blackboard and one full hour of writing and erasing, with lines here and there, and additions and subtractions, they came up with what they felt to be a manageable timetable and calendar. (See Table 2.)

The calendar was predicated on two demands: the sense of outline and pacing. People liked to know when something began and where it ended, and that the middle—the actual time of the solicitations—was intense but brief, and especially, that the whole process would not drag on interminably. Having meetings clustered around the weekends gave the necessary time during midweek to do the work as prescribed by the meetings. Finally, highlights of the process could be presented on Sundays, as a constant reminder to the parishioners.

The time schedule was the best they could do. They worried that some volunteers would drop out along the way, but it was a good schedule and vital guide. They would go with it. Copies would be mimeographed for all the key workers.

There was one last item: job descriptions for the chairmen. By turns, the chairmen discussed their duties. There were two reasons for doing this. Each chairman had to be sure about what he or she was to do. Everyone else had to be sure of the duties, so there would be no overlapping. The clearer each person was about the process, the clearer it would be to everyone else.[29]

The Proposal chairman, Vic Verve, was first. He would make sure there would be a clearly drawn statement of purpose for the parish. He would make certain that as many people would be brought into the Proposal design as possible. A true estimate of actual and potential membership would be part of the Proposal. Yes, he would attend all the necessary meetings, and he would get a committee of at least six persons to assist him.

The Communications chairman, Curt Conflict, was next. He

would make sure all the materials were prepared and distributed to the necessary people. He would answer such questions as who gets what and when and why. And this would come after he designed and executed exactly what was to be distributed. And at this stage, he didn't want any jerk telling him how to do his job.

The Special Events chairman, Pat Pious, followed. There were going to be a number of services, dinners, and other gatherings connected with the effort, and it would be the responsibility of Pat to make sure everything was done in the right way.

The Contact chairman, Pauline Politic, said she would recruit the leaders for the person-to-person visits and make sure they knew what they were going to speak about to people.

The Rector, followed by the Senior Warden, pledged his support to Joe Joiner; and, at Joe's insistence, the three of them agreed to act as what they called a Committee of Leaders.

Joe also stated his specific responsibilities. As chairman of the Renewal Committee, he would oversee the complete thing —dates, people, agendas, schedules, contacts, materials, distribution, follow through. He would even be the chief spokesman for the effort, and the chief recipient of all the complaints. Whether it was right or wrong, productive or otherwise, he would become the symbol of the success or failure of the campaign. He would be either the hero or the bum.

They were off and running, hopefully in the same race and on the same track, with the same finishing line.

MORE PREPARATIONS

The next week arrived and, with it, a major problem of getting volunteers.

It was time to enlist three area leaders. The Vestry's analysis indicated that the parish reached into three distinct areas of the community. The north and west side (area #1), which represented the wealthier; the south and east side (area #2), which had the apartments housing mostly the elderly and the younger families; and the inner-town (area #3), which had the minorities and more elderly, plus singles.

Joe asked Angie Angry and Skip Skeptic to be area leaders, and both refused. He suspected that their noses were out of joint for not being made chairmen of the four key committees but he let it go at that. They would, perhaps, be willing to help later on, especially if he did not antagonize them right now. Three vestrymen, thanks to the telephoning of the warden, agreed to take the positions.

The four key committees were meeting.

The Proposal Committee of three, plus the Rector and the Senior Warden who sat with them, had to hold the reins on Vic Verve who still wanted to move too fast with insufficient information. After some tugging, Vic agreed that the heads of the various parish organizations would be contacted in the next two days to find out exactly what their plans were for the next year, and, therefore, what they wanted in the proposal itself which would strengthen their hand.

The Communications Committee started calling the local printing shops to get an idea of how much more forty-pound mimeograph stock cost than the thinner twenty-pound stock normally used for parish communications. Curt Conflict called the librarian of the local library and told her that it was her duty to donate her talents for the design of a brochure, especially since her mother had always been a member of the parish. The librarian, who by the way was a freelance artist, told Curt what he could do with his arrogance, and slammed the telephone receiver down. Curt decided he could do it himself, and spent the next four hours making sketches on some colored poster paper. One of Curt's committee members started making phone calls to find out what pledge cards other churches were using, and collected a number of samples.

The three couples who had been part of the prayer group comprised Pat Pious's Special Events Committee. Their first idea was to plan a special service in the church for a month hence, which would open the campaign. Their second plan of action was to assign two of their number to make a detailed tour of the parish hall to see just how many people they could fit in and feed in the event they wanted to have some kind of dinner.

The Contact Committee, under Pauline Politic's guidance, avoided facing the fact that most of the people they were to visit had years of built-in resistance patterns. Fearing failure, Pauline did not call a meeting of the committee until late in the week, and then only at the constant urging of Joe.

Joe reassured her by quoting from a study he had read: "A parish is frequently composed of a core of responsive individuals surrounded by groups of people of lesser degrees of involvement, and of spots or clusters of people with whom the parish finds it difficult to deal by reason of estrangement for one or another reason."[30]

"So," asked Pauline, "we're just like every other parish?"

"I'm afraid so," Joe answered, hoping Pauline would not think he was being totally negative. "And that," he continued, "is our challenge, I guess. A challenge to make us more than the average." Pauline smiled knowingly, and Joe was pleased to find himself so personally motivated that he could give an impromptu pep talk. Wait until he told this to Betty.

Trouble

Curt Conflict and Vic Verve wanted a meeting with Joe, the Rector, and the Senior Warden, right away.

BEYOND PLEDGING

Curt and Vic had met after church the previous Sunday, and they came to the conclusion that the parishioners, the few of them who were attending church these days, looked tired, and busy. Would they be able to enlist enough people to make an extensive house-to-house campaign?

Curt had a plan. He was an executive of an advertising company, and a good one too. He would write a letter explaining the parish's problem in detail, and stating the needs in clear, concise and provocative prose, and even include a pledge card. He would not stop there, of course. In two weeks he would have his secretary compile a list of those who did not respond, and these people would receive a second letter, a little more harsh in tone but, nevertheless, straight to the point about the real need for pledges from *all* the parishioners. And yes indeed, he would even go a step further, and compose a letter of thanks which would go out over the Rector's signature.

Vic Verve was quick to back this up. "Look," Vic said, "Curt here has all sorts of experience in direct-mail campaigns and could do this. Besides, it would make everyone else feel less pressured about giving so much time. Why waste so much time with all these weeks, if we can accomplish the same thing in a series of letters written by a real pro? Don't you agree?"

The Senior Warden was first to respond, and in anger. "You can't change horses in midstream. We agreed on a procedure, and you have no right to put a monkey wrench in the works."

Curt raised his eyebrows. "Aren't you mixing a few too many metaphors in your own verbal cocktail?"

The warden's face turned livid. "What in God's name do metaphors have to do with it?

"Perhaps more than you'll ever know," answered Curt.

Joe stepped in. "Hey, friends, can I get a word in here?"

The warden was too involved. "Sure, as long as it's poetic," he said sarcastically.

"Intelligent style never hurt anyone," added Curt for what he felt was good measure."

"Gentlemen, gentlemen!" the Rector said. "Let's hear what Joe has to say."

What Joe had to say was that although Curt and Vic had a point, they had all agreed to follow the more personal approach, and it was wrong to change it now. Curt wanted to interrupt, but Joe motioned for silence to let him finish. "Look," Joe concluded, "this campaign is more than just bringing in a few extra dollars. It has to do with, well, with revival of the parish, which can't always be measured in dollars and cents."

Curt remained combative. "Oh, we're now talking about revival? You mean that stamping-the-feet-and-shouting-alleluias-and-dancing-in-a-circle-around-town-holding-hands is going to pay the electric bill? Who're you kidding?"

"Okay, okay"—Joe wanted to stop the argument—"I'm not going to argue the value or meaning of revival at the moment. I am saying, however, that we all agreed—and that goes for you too—that our committee was to be called *Renewal* not because it sounded fancier, but because it spoke of the real need in this parish."

"And what was that?" Curt wanted to know.

"To get out of the doldrums. To rub the sand from the eyes. To stretch the limbs and rise from the deathbed. . . . Hey, Curt," Joe added with a friendly smile, "how am I doing with the metaphors?"

Curt, caught off guard, smiled too. "Not bad." Then the smile disappeared. "For an amateur."

Joe had had enough of this guy. "As long as I'm responsible for this Renewal Committee, I insist that we go with our original plan of making the contacts as personal as can be. To stop short of that, with letters only, will merely lead to disaster. That's the way its going to be, like it or lump it."

With that, the discussion ended. It was a stand-off.

All week, Joe kicked himself for pulling rank at the last minute. He believed he was right. In the past, the parish had taken the easy way out, hiding behind letters and gentle appeals from the steps of the chancel—and peeling paint, terrible attendance, and bored choir were the results. Joe was right, but he regretted not being able to mitigate the obvious irritation between Curt and the Senior Warden. In the weeks ahead, he would have to mend fences, clasp hands in friendship, tie the knots that bind, or whatever metaphor applied to the pleasure and pains of life in this family.

IT TAKES PEOPLE

During the two weeks of preparation for the actual outreach to the parish community, Joe was called upon to referee a number of disputes, such as the one between Curt Conflict and the warden.

As Betty and Joe compared notes during their few free moments, Betty suddenly asked, "Joe, why *did* you accept the chairmanship?"

"Why? . . . I took the assignment for, who knows, for a million reasons. I was flattered at being asked, and I wanted to try my wings at being, well, at being king for a day."

"And now," Betty said, after a pause, "you're finding out that kings, at least the kings in this town, don't get a chance to sit on cushioned thrones high up on the rooftops."

The Lesson

Joe, always being called down from his rooftop, went back to some notes he had made while reading about leadership.

One quotation seemed especially significant: "Leadership is 'interpersonal influence, exercised in situations and directed, through the communication process, toward the attainment of a specified goal or goals. Leadership always invokes attempts on the part of a leader (influencer) to affect (influence) the behavior of a follower (influencee) or followers in the situation.' "[31] Joe knew he could never do all that while perched high above the human comedy.

Answering this question and preventing that conflict gave Joe little time to theorize during the next few weeks of preparation. One particular request came from the Treasurer, who gave the Proposal Committee a chart showing percentage giving as it relates to weekly income. (See Table 3.)

The Proposal Committee was grateful to receive the data, but an argument grew out of a plea by the Treasurer to have the chart mailed to every parishioner immediately.

Joe asked to meet with the Treasurer and Vic Verve, chairman of the Proposal Committee, to see if this could be straightened out before the next meeting of the committee.

The Treasurer's argument was essentially this: The terrible performance of giving in this parish means that we can no longer baby these people. This is a good time to hit each of them, smack in the face, with this chart. Then there won't be any question about what each member is giving versus what each member could be giving. Vic's argument was essentially this: These members are not stupid. They know exactly what they are giving and refusing to give. This chart indicts them in a public way, and the people might rebel by refusing to consider any new proposal, concluding that it was a cover-up for a hard-sell campaign for more cash, and only more cash.

"Well, what do you think it is?" the Treasurer asked, when Vic concluded.

They were off and running again. Joe, then Vic tried their best to convince the Treasurer that the Renewal Committee

Table 3
GUIDE FOR GIVING

Weekly Income	3%	4%	5%	6%	7%	8%	9%	Biblical Tithe	15%
$ 50	$ 1.50	$ 2.00	$ 2.50	$ 3.00	$ 3.50	$ 4.00	$ 4.50	$ 5.00	$ 7.50
$ 75	2.25	3.00	3.75	4.50	5.25	6.00	6.75	7.50	11.25
$ 100	3.00	4.00	5.00	6.00	7.00	8.00	9.00	10.00	15.00
$ 150	4.50	6.00	7.50	9.00	10.50	12.00	13.50	15.00	22.50
$ 200	6.00	8.00	10.00	12.00	14.00	16.00	18.00	20.00	30.00
$ 250	7.50	10.00	12.50	15.00	17.50	20.00	22.50	25.00	37.50
$ 300	9.00	12.00	15.00	18.00	21.00	24.00	27.00	30.00	45.00
$ 350	10.50	14.00	17.50	21.00	24.50	28.00	31.50	35.00	52.50
$ 400	12.00	16.00	20.00	24.00	28.00	32.00	36.00	40.00	60.00
$ 450	13.50	18.00	22.50	27.00	31.50	36.00	40.50	45.00	67.50
$ 500	15.00	20.00	25.00	30.00	35.00	40.00	45.00	50.00	75.00
$ 550	16.50	22.00	27.50	33.00	38.50	44.00	49.50	55.00	82.50
$ 600	18.00	24.00	30.00	36.00	42.00	48.00	54.00	60.00	90.00
$ 650	19.50	26.00	32.50	39.00	45.50	52.00	58.50	65.00	97.50
$ 700	21.00	28.00	35.00	42.00	49.00	56.00	63.00	70.00	105.00
$ 750	22.50	30.00	37.50	45.00	52.50	60.00	67.50	75.00	112.50
$ 800	24.00	32.00	40.00	48.00	56.00	64.00	72.00	80.00	120.00
$ 850	25.50	34.00	42.50	51.00	59.50	68.00	76.50	85.00	127.50
$ 900	27.00	36.00	45.00	54.00	63.00	72.00	81.00	90.00	135.00
$ 950	28.50	38.00	47.50	57.00	66.50	76.00	85.50	95.00	142.50
$1000	30.00	40.00	50.00	60.00	70.00	80.00	90.00	100.00	150.00

ONE VIEW FROM THE PEW 59

had more to do than run after cash, but the Treasurer, who had been in the parish longer than the two of them, said, "Tell me that when I have to pay salaries next month," and he walked away.

That evening Joe and Vic talked about it some more on the telephone. There was hope. Vic seemed less impetuous, and Joe was feeling more at home within the whole process. They were learning. And there seemed to be a compromise solution to the chart problem whereby copies would be available to canvassers, as reference material, but it would not be mailed out to the entire parish.

Whether or not each member of the Renewal Committee knew it, they were learning many things about the church and themselves and each other. Four things especially:

First, "the characteristics of group goals and their relation to the attractiveness and productivity of a committee." *Second*, "the effect of member acceptance and rejection upon the way in which people communicated within the group and upon the group problem-solving procedures." *Third*, "the necessary membership functions related to accomplishing group tasks and to building the interpersonal relationships which would be necessary for group effectiveness." *Fourth*, "the steps involved in program planning and goal formation."[32]

Joe, as leader, had to concentrate on making the Renewal Committee work, and work well, but his concern was wider than that. He had to keep in focus the complex interpersonal and group experiences which each day brought.

Joe recalled another point in his reading. His committee had its meaning in the fact that, for each of them in the parish, this experience "would increase the sensitivity of committee members to one another and to the process and problems of their own group development."[33] It was a matter of mutuality between the influencer, the influencee, and the variety of influences from the parishioners whom he met on the way to the supermarket, the movies, and the altar.

THIRD WEEK

During the next weeks when the Renewal Committee made its move, it relied heavily on a number of items. The first was the regular meetings between the three key people and, second, the relationship of the whole effort to that which was said and done in church on Sunday.

Pat Pious's Special Events Committee played down the kick-off-dinner idea because the old stove could not be relied on for anything more than heating some water for a pot of coffee. The guilds had stopped functioning years ago. It was just that the few elderly ladies who met every month did not know it yet.

If no dinners for the parish, then what? Through its worship, that corporate act of belonging, being, and doing.

Pat's committee went over one of the key assumptions made about the work of the parish; namely, developing the life of the parish community as a fellowship with mutual concerns both within and outside its membership. This started with the Sunday event, those few hours on Sunday morning. That is where the parish provided the atmosphere and action for corporate witness to what they believed it was all about.

The Special Events Committee discussed this with the Rector, Joe, and the Senior Warden. They went over the calendar again, in more detail this time. The six Sunday events were crucial. The first had dealt with the *Nature of Church Membership*, a personalization of the Canons of the church. On the second Sunday the Rector had made the *Initial Announcement of the Renewal Committee* and the effort in general. This third week demanded a statement and words and action dealing with the *Theology of Stewardship*.

The Rector asked if the prayer group would like to design an order of service. They would not, but they would like to take part in the regular service. This was the start of a fuller use of lay readers in the parish.

The usual attendance on Sundays was poor, so they were not reaching a decent percentage of the membership. They discussed possible ways to increase attendance since, at this point, they had no money to send weekly announcements about the Renewal effort. They would have to drum up business for Sunday worship.

They would telephone the parishioners. But all three hundred of them, including the inactives? Who had time for that? Pat's committee decided that no one had the time to reach all of them, but some of them could reach a few. And that's what they did. Each member of the committee took ten names, and called them.

The purpose of the telephone message was simple. It was to announce that on Sunday next the Rector would tell them about a theory of stewardship as a preparation for their Renewal efforts this year. They hoped this simple, direct method would work.

Other Problems

While Pat's committee was telephoning, Curt Conflict was getting estimates the likes of which had never been seen in the parish before. Curt showed his committee a number of elaborate designs for brochures, plus some small advertisements for the local papers. The members of his committee were intimi-

62   BEYOND PLEDGING

dated by the performance, and Joe wanted to kick himself for not putting some limits to Curt's creative energies.

"Do you want it to look good, or not?" asked Curt.

"We want," Joe answered, "the best we can get, for the money."

"I know that!" Curt was mad. "But I also know you have to spend money to make money. Anyone knows that. Even you!"

Curt was right, and wrong. But, more importantly, Joe had erred in not drawing a budget for expenses. Curt's ideas were great but they were too expensive. If they were to spend all the money Curt's designs demanded there would be nothing for anything else. The Treasurer surely would never meet the payroll. Joe tried to explain all this to Curt.

"Then you should have told me how much I could spend," admonished Curt, "and right from the start, so I wouldn't have wasted so much time."

Joe admitted that Curt was right. Joe should have established the budget for the campaign. He did not know why such a fundamental item had been neglected, but it had. Curt was not the only one who would be operating in a financial vacuum. Joe was so busy thinking about the new goals of the congregation that he had neglected to think about, or get others to think about, the budget necessities of the campaign.

And More

Meanwhile, the Contact Committee was having big trouble. One out of every five people solicited said that they might, just might, be able to volunteer to be Callers. Pauline, as polite as could be, tried to explain what a feather in their cap it would be to take part in this campaign. Most of those who refused were also polite, except for two disinterested parishioners who told her they had no caps. One man, called to the telephone in the middle of an argument with his teenage son, told Pauline where she could stick the feather, then hung up.

The form for the proposal was simple, direct, and reduced to one page for easy handling. (See Table 4.)

The proposal was finalized, not on Monday as they planned but on Friday, at the special meeting of the seven-member cabinet plus the six members of the Proposal Committee. Vic Verve presented their recommendations in mimeographed form, which was a blessing. They could study the proposal as a group.

It was decided to go with the simple statement of program and budget, and mimeograph sufficient copies for distribution on Sunday morning in church.

Who would present the proposal in church? Pauline thought the Rector should do it. Everyone else thought Joe should do it. He thought he should too, but he caught himself before saying so. Something told him to hold back. It might be better for him to wait until the end of the campaign to make his statement. It might be wiser for the Rector to call upon Vic Verve as chairman of the Proposal Committee to read and explain the proposal and budget. Yes, everyone agreed that this was a better idea. Vic was very pleased, and said he would do his best. Joe felt he had done something right for a change.

It was late in the third week, and they were behind schedule. The proposal was mailed on Saturday, five days later than planned, which meant that it would not arrive at the homes of the parishioners until early into the fourth week.

What they were mailing infuriated Curt Conflict, but delighted his committee who by now, for all practical purposes, had gone home to forget the whole thing. They wanted nothing to do with Curt and his fancy designs. To mail simple mimeographed sheets was, to Curt, stupid and insulting. He wondered why they needed him in the first place. Joe took two deep

Table 4
FORM FOR A BUDGET PROPOSAL

Our Hopes for Mission:	Budget: 197__	Actual: 197__	Proposed: 197__
Worship and Education: What it involves to provide the primary function of the parish (no personnel)	$	$	
Details of any modifications needed for the new year (sum added or subtracted from the totals above)			$ ......
Parochial Activities: A description of the basic pastoral services provided for its parishioners	$	$	
Details of any adjustments to the above			$ ......
Community Activities: What the parish does in and for the local community	$	$	
Details of any adjustments to the above			$ ......
A Larger Outreach: What the parish does with the diocese and general church program	$	$	
Details of any adjustments to the above			$ ......
Personnel: What it costs in terms of staff, salaries, and benefits, to perform the necessary parochial work	$	$	
Details of any adjustments to the above			$ ......
Administration: What the parish needs in terms of materials and supplies	$	$	

Details of any adjustments to the above .... $ ......

Property: This gives details of mortgages, utilities, and items for maintenance ..... $ ...... $ ......

Details of any adjustments to the above .... $ ......

Miscellaneous: This is the catch-all section .... $ ...... $ ......

Details of any adjustments to the above .... $ ......

Totals: $ _____ $ _____ $ _____

Our Hopes for Support:	Actual: 197__	Our Need: 197__
Regular Support: Details of what pledging is and how it works	$	$ ......
Loose Plate Offering: An explanation of how this differs from pledges	$	$ ......
Church School: The reason for having the children use envelopes	$	$ ......
Special Offerings: Details of any seasonal or special request for additional funds ..	$	$ ......
Investments: Endowments and other sources of investment income	$	$ ......
Contributions: Details of monies from use of property, and other special offerings ..	$	$ ......
Totals:	$ _____	$ _____

breaths and apologized again. Curt was bugging Joe and the once happy and carefree tennis buff wanted to tell Curt that the reason they needed him was to demonstrate how ridiculous a big, fancy campaign would have been. Joe did not say this, however. Joe was not sure if he were not just a little jealous of Curt's ability to design. Joe, the architect, had a few artistic prizes up his own sleeve. Perhaps Joe had wanted to push his own plans. Joe considered this seriously. He decided that his own hidden agendas might very well have triggered a few of the fights. Yes, it looked as if . . . Joe stopped this line of thought. He was ill-equipped to be a psychologist. But, as he remarked to his wife later that night, it was an interesting theory to think about nevertheless.

Saturday was a hectic day. The Callers were to be trained and Pauline Politic did her best, but she bent over backward to make it so easy on the volunteers that Vic Verve had to barge in to give them one of his better pep talks about when the going gets tough get going, and other red-hot charges.

To everyone's surprise, Angie Angry and Skip Skeptic turned up for the Callers' meeting, and were made captains on the spot.

Now for the initial gifts. It was mandatory, they felt, to present the proposal on Sunday. It was also necessary, they felt, to announce a few major gifts at the same time. This was a mistake. Joe, along with the Senior Warden and the Treasurer, called a number of key persons from area 1, the wealthier north and west side, asking for major gifts as an incentive. Three out of the ten families called said they were perfectly willing to do it, but requested that their names not be mentioned.

They frantically called each of the Vestry and the committee chairmen. Would these individuals make a pledge now so their commitment could be announced on Sunday? This was successful. They were able to secure ninety percent pledges, with fifty percent of them slightly higher than the previous year. Joe and the warden decided that they would announce the fact that ninety percent had pledged and ignore the fact that only fifty percent were willing to increase the amount over last year.

The present program of the parish was dull. The proposal they would be presenting the following week was not world-shaking, but neither was it dull. It suggested an outreach into the community with a few extended programs. The choir would sing at the local hospital, the youth would give a workday once a month, they would increase their pledge to the diocesan projects hitherto ignored, audio visual equipment would be purchased for the educational program which, by the way, would be expanded to include special classes for the elderly on weekdays and for the prayer group. On one hand, the increased activities were not much, and the costs were limited to twenty-five percent above the low budget of the previous two years, but it was a start in the right direction.

Joe was happy. So far so good.

CONTACT

The fourth week of the six-week campaign to move the parish from the doldrums of apathy to what the committee hoped would approach a vivacious renaissance, started with high hopes and ended in creeping pessimism.

On Sunday the proposal was distributed, and at the time usually allowed for the sermon it was presented in fifteen breathless minutes by a nervous but determined Vic Verve. It met with mixed responses. Joe noticed that some parishioners who expected an exegesis of the Gospel appointed for the day were annoyed. Others who wanted to ask questions could not, and they seemed to be more annoyed. Most of the parishioners at both services, however, welcomed the information, and remarked later at the coffee hour that it was the first time they had been given a chance to get a feel for the whole thing. Yes, they liked what they heard in the proposal and they would do what they could to support it.

Joe was unable to estimate the reaction when the Rector announced that ninety percent of the Vestry and committee chairmen had made their pledges already. It seemed to Joe that the comments he heard that day centered not around the ninety-percent supporters but, rather, on the resistant ten-percenters.

He had to answer questions about the ten-percenters. No, they were not the recalcitrants. Yes, they were still members of the parish. No, they were not angry. Yes, they would make their pledges before too long. No, Joe was not disappointed. Yes, Joe was hopeful. Yes, indeed, all leaders were subject to questions, yes indeed. No, leaders did not enjoy all of the questions.

On Monday the contacts by the Captains and their Callers began. On Tuesday twenty percent of the parish had been contacted. By Wednesday ten percent of the Callers had dropped away, and the Captains were carrying on. By Thursday Joe, the Senior Warden, and the committee chairmen were making calls. By Friday evening, seventy-five percent of the parish had been contacted, and the pledges were only forty percent of what had been expected. By Saturday they had reached eighty percent of the parish, and had received pledges from sixty-five percent of those reached. And that was that for the fourth week.

Fifth Week

The Senior Warden announced the results of the contacts at the services on the fifth Sunday of the campaign: Of the eighty percent called upon, sixty-five percent pledged five percent more than last year's budget. More calls would be made during the first part of the fifth week. The warden should have stopped right there, but he didn't. What followed was a vociferous outpouring of reasons why the parish should be ashamed of itself for such a terrible response to the efforts of so many hard-working people who had given so much of their time.

Twenty minutes later the Senior Warden finished his tirade, and the Rector moved swiftly into the sermon hymn—but almost everyone was still feeling the tongue lashing. The hymn singing was a feeble effort, as was the sermon that followed. Almost no one stayed for the coffee hour. Not until then did the warden realize his error.

"Well, Joe," lamented the Senior Warden, "I guess I botched things up for you this time."

"You gave them just what they deserved," interrupted the Treasurer, who patted the Senior Warden on the back. "It's time," he continued, "that someone gave them the business."

Joe's disappointment prevented him from making any comment. He just hung his head, patted the warden on the back, reached for another cup of coffee, and dreamed of springtime and tennis.

"Well," said the warden, "now you know why I failed to come forth when the Rector first asked for a chairman. I've been in this post for so many years I'm locked into old attitudes."

During the next four days, a strenuous effort was made to secure pledges from the rest of the parish, but it did not succeed. Everyone was tired, some tired of banging on doors in the community and others tired of having their door touched even in the slightest way.

Adjustments

The cabinet met on Friday night of the fifth week. Joe presided over a disappointed group of seven. The program and budget plans for the next year had to be reduced.

They went back to *priorities*. What were the few essentials regarding the life of this parish? What items could be cut altogether? Which of them could be restored at a later time, if and when monies were available?

"Ah, I have it!" said Pauline Politic. "If we present two budgets, then no one will be disappointed."

They asked her what she meant by two budgets. To her it meant an *actual* budget which would be in line with the pledges; and also a *potential* budget which would list all the possibilities as a kind of reminder of what life and work in the parish could be like if, well, if more people responded with increased giving.

It was an interesting idea all right, but after much debate, it was decided to cut the program and budget to make it no more than five percent over the pledges.

The leaders of the Renewal Committee mimeographed the revised program and budget for distribution on Sunday, and went home for a relaxing Saturday away from church matters.

Sixth Week

Joe was the speaker on the sixth Sunday. He presented the revised program and budget as realistic but full of promise. In the middle of his brief talk he used the catch phrase *New Hope Awakes* absentmindedly, but it rang true to him, so he used it twice more before he finished.

The program for the new year had three extra items in it. It was not as much as they had planned but, still, three more particular programs than last year. The budget would be six percent higher than last year, not much in view of inflationary realities but, still, ahead of last year. The parish was moving ahead. There was hope.

The Rector thanked the workers for their extraordinary efforts on behalf of the parish; and the genuineness of his comments was felt by everyone.

A dinner meeting was planned for Friday night for the whole Renewal Committee. There would be time allotted for a free exchange of comments about what was right and wrong with the six-week effort. On Saturday, Joe would meet with the six others in his cabinet to summarize and evaluate the various comments. This performance evaluation was necessary, but, as Joe sat, tired and disappointed, in his den, it seemed threatening to him personally.

THERE'S ALWAYS NEXT YEAR

On Saturday, as scheduled, the following members of the parish met with Joe: the Rector, the Senior Warden, Pauline, Pat, Curt, and Vic. This was the cabinet, the core group whose task was to offer recommendations for next year's efforts to raise money for program and budget in the parish.

The previous night had brought many comments from the full committee, and these would be analyzed. Comments from the parishioners in general, such as: It didn't mean enough to those calling on others. The parish was too far gone anyway.

Do we need all these churches? Why doesn't the parish teach the Ten Commandments anymore? I kinda like the revised Prayer Book. If you use that Green Book anymore I'm leaving for good. There's not enough for the kids. They think more about the kids than the old folks. We'd like to do more but with the children off to school, well, you know how it is. The choir sings the same hymns week after week. And on and on.

More practical concerns were expressed. Two families had offered to sign over their *insurance policies* and the committee members did not know how to deal with this offer in specific ways other than say thanks and hand the matter over to an insurance salesman for explanation. Many persons thought that wills should be discussed openly but no one had planned for that. Someone thought that all the Episcopal churches in the general area should combine forces and do things together, or at least *combine purchase* of equipment and supplies from the same wholesaler, thereby deriving a better discount. Others said that if the church leaders were smart enough to make better use of *volunteers* then the budget could be cut considerably.

Generally, the effort to contact each parish family paid off. Those who had not been contacted for some time felt that someone cared, even if it was just for some money. The sense of caring was a major step in the right direction. Almost everyone was glad to know that the parish was alive enough to have such a campaign. The Renewal Committee had success, and about sixty percent of them said they would be willing to serve on the committee next year.

One unanimous query was: Why had they failed to apply the sound business methods in the parish that they applied in every other enterprise? By instinct they knew how to do things efficiently. Then why did they ignore it in the parish?

The summary from the cabinet centered on four items: *time* (there was never enough), *people* (never enough of the right ones at the right time), *expenses* (never enough to do what was necessary), *ownership*. The fourth item was as serious as the others, but it was more difficult to identify.

Ownership

Joe understood ownership as well as the next person. Owning something was personal, serious, and loving. It suggested embracing and holding fast that which was vital to oneself. And if all that meant anything to Joe, it meant that he had some kind of an ongoing commitment to that which he owned. He would defend and protect what he owned. He would also take care to present what he owned in the best possible light.

Thinking of the words "best possible light" reminded Joe of his own home. He had chopped down two big, sickly trees right in front, just to give the entrance-way more light and attractiveness. The house was their home. His family lived there in comfort, and he did what was necessary to keep it comfortable. They enjoyed it, and wanted their friends to enjoy it too. They took pains to keep up the grounds. It was important to them.

The idea about ownership had been introduced by the only teenager on the Renewal Committee. She had *questioned whether or not enough parishioners really felt an ownership in the process of renewal in this or any church these days*. It was a casual offhand comment but it stirred up heated discussion. Her point was that, not unlike the houseowner, anyone who claimed membership in any organization was merely a joiner unless he or she became personally involved, willing to do all that was necessary to make the organization prosper.

What did "ownership of the parish" mean to parishioners? Was it enthusiasm for life and purpose? The determining spirit? The will to live? At this point in the discussion Pat Pious reminded them of the theme *New Hope Awakes*, introduced by Joe.

"It's a mighty effective slogan," Curt Conflict agreed.

"Are we interested in mere slogans?" asked the Senior Warden as he looked directly at Curt.

Joe did not want another fight between these two men, so he took an informal vote right then and there. The question before them was: Would it be valuable to consider a theme for this and next year centered around the optimistic thought that a sense of new hope really does awaken people?

Curt wanted the floor. "Don't you think," he demanded, "that we should discuss this before rushing into a vote?"

The battery of jeers for Curt and cheers for Joe demonstrated how completely Curt had antagonized the committee. The vote was unanimous, save for Curt's abstention. They would recommend a procedure for next year under the heading of *New Hope Awakes*.

Decision Making

The Renewal Committee learned the hard way that only through orderly process could meaningful decisions be made. They drew a plan for a cyclical, four-part process. (See Table 5.)

The first step, *Preparation*, was easy to ignore, especially when one was faced with the urgency of deadlines or, worse, the crisis of imminent financial disaster. The temptation to "get on with it" was always great, but it could be deadly. An ill-conceived plan without the benefit of knowledge of the subject will fail, but, what was equally important, the organization might never have the chance to try it again. To be

Table 5
THE FOUR BASICS OF DECISION MAKING
I Preparation

1. Determine, via an honest self-analysis, what the problem really is and where you are within it
2. Gather data in light of this analysis
   a) Programs, religious and secular
   b) Economics and resources available
   c) Environment and demographics; who is who and why
   d) Attitudes, ethos, willingness
   e) The nature of the leadership
3. Transcribe these data into workable information
4. Make assumptions (detailed analysis) about the future

II Proposal

5. Determine where you want to go in view of hopes and realities
6. Consider the alternates, using models for testing
7. Design the proposal to say exactly what you want it to say

III Pursuance

8. Selling the decision to the various publics
9. Carrying out these decisions

IV Perusal

10. Review, via self-analysis with a willingness to begin all over again

---

judged by others as having sloppy, faulty management and preparation was to be turned down no matter how worthy the would-be organizers thought their project was. As a successful architect, Joe knew that his projects consisted of seventy-five percent thought and twenty-five percent drawing. The portrait painter and the playwright could say the same thing; so could the chief executive officer of every major industry.

Gathering hard facts could be dull because it was so routine. Changing the data into workable information, however, could be very creative. For example, it might not be the most exciting event in one's life to find out how many persons living in the parish between the ages of eight and eighteen had hearing problems. The numbers represent data. Going the next step, however, and finding out how many of these young people might want special training approaches to communication (perhaps even including sign language) opens up all sorts of possibilities in terms of audio-visual and other programs. The combination of certain data into programmatic information is part of the first and very crucial step in decision making.

The second step, *Proposal*, was the content of decision making. Did the parish want to be big, and grow bigger? Did it want to remain small? There would come a time when parishes would be free enough from intimidating statistics to propose a smaller membership doing a very specific ministry. What would the information tell about the particular parish— where the parish had to go or where you and some of your friends would like to see it go? There is a difference which, unfortunately, too many often overlook.

To consider the alternatives was mandatory. The point to remember was that to study alternatives meant to take a closer look at the proposal itself.

The proposal had to be good communication. The art of communication was saying the right thing to the right person for the right response. It was an art because it rarely happened, but when it did, others felt it to the tips of their nerve endings. A good proposal was good communication when it detailed the plan. Exactly. Clearly. Refreshingly stimulating.

The third step was *Pursuance*. There was a danger at this step to allow the proposal to stand on its own merits without the necessary expenditure of further time and talent. This was understandable. The people behind the proposal were often exhausted from the efforts in the first two steps, and frequently felt it was the obligation of the recipient to take over from there. Usually this did not happen. Simply put, a proposal is proposed over and over again.

The decisions, as outlined in the proposal, were still merely words and ideas. They took shape only when they were carried out by those who designed the proposal in the first place.

The fourth step, *Perusal*, prepared the decision maker to begin all over again in this four-part cyclical process. This step dealt with the task of a careful reading of the whole process in an attempt to understand what went right and what went wrong. Evaluation was difficult. But no matter how painful, a complete review was an absolute must.

Did any process ever end? Some of Joe's cabinet thought so, but usually it did not. This fourth step was, perhaps, the first one after all, the real beginning for the next effort. If seen as such, the less pain and drudgery, the greater the opportunities for creative thinking.

There were variations on these four steps in the decision-making process, and each parish would have to find its own, but, for this parish at this time, it was the recommended procedure. It was a guide.

Leadership

Joe Joiner was tired but happy. The campaign, which he would continue to label *New Hope Awakes*, was over. There were some successes, and many suggestions for improvement. He had learned much about the parish and its fellow members.

The parish had a long way to go. The paint was still chipping, and the boiler was repaired rather than replaced. But there were other signs too. It seemed that more people were freer to speak about the parish, and even speak about it in spiritual terms. Including Joe.

Joe was honest enough to admit that, in his past, he had been a joiner of things for no reason other than joining. He could not say no, and he liked to belong. The Episcopal Church was something to belong to, for reasons he never cared to explore.

Joe had said some things in his reports that he never thought he would feel, let alone say. Statements such as: The aim of the parish is to glorify God by worshiping Him according to His word, by doing His will in our daily lives, and by sharing with others the gospel of salvation through faith in the Lord Jesus Christ. Joe admitted that Pat Pious and the Rector had helped him with the words but, what was very important, before this campaign he would have been too embarrassed even to whisper the words to himself. So this was a start.

Joe Joiner wanted to be a leader, and a good one. This campaign had given him a fine start. So, in his den that night, Joe got out a yellow pad and pencil and asked himself a series of questions about leadership. These questions, appropriately, began with the probing word "would," expressing what might be expected of him.

Would he have proficiency? Did he know the faith? Would he read books on the subject? Would he be willing to go beyond the Canons for information? Would he go to church enough?

Would he be willing to think? Would he allow for inspiration? Would he be watchful for impetuosity? Would he consider alternatives?

Would he know the condition? Would he work in accordance with the church's structure and capabilities? Would he know where the church was at? Would he knew what this cliché meant to a variety of people unlike himself?

Would he know people and systems? Would he see the details of interpersonal relationships from a larger perspective? Would he investigate the wheels of process? Would he attempt to discover what an organization was, and means?

Would he develop and witness to a sense of destiny? Would he be able to discern the demands for being a witness within the holy community, to function in a holy history? Would he hide behind pious phrases only?

Would he seek the larger will? Would he be willing to separate his own agenda from that of the organization's? Would he seek the mind of God in prayer and elsewhere?

Would he make timely decisions? Would he have the courage to act whenever necessary? Would he be willing to take the responsibilities for such actions?

Would he set an example? Would he make a constant effort to reflect the glory of God? Would he say and do what he wanted others to say and do?

Would he follow through? Would he ensure that the tasks were understood, supervised, and accomplished? Would he avoid leaving unfinished projects hanging in midair?

Would he evaluate constantly? Would he have the nerve to measure his own performance? Would he allow others to do it?

It took Joe Joiner two days to get over the trauma of this bombardment of questions. He did not need anyone to tell him that the questions, numerous as they were, reflected a thousand more questions just over the horizon. Did he really have the time for his church? He was too busy. Who needed the aggravation? It was a pain in the neck. It exhausted him to think of it.

During the rest of the week, however, curiosity got the best of Joe, and he read some more, and considered all the words used to describe the characteristics of leadership.

There was *attitude*: as evidenced by cooperation, motivation, sincerity, unselfishness, enthusiasm, desire to assist others, attention to details, tact, and a thorough willingness to assume responsibility.

There was *force*: as evidenced by ability to organize and command, decisiveness, self-confidence, poise, drive, aggressiveness, determination and moral courage, and ability to delegate authority.

There was *dependability*: as evidenced by initiative, promptness, consistency, judgment, clear thinking, acting without supervision, pursuing a course of action to successful completion, perseverance, and absolute loyalty to the church he served.

There was *bearing*: as evidenced by his appearance and deportment, ability to roll with the punches, have courtesy, plus a sensitivity for genuine laughter and joy.

Joe doubted he could ever live up to all those standards, but they were good guides that might come in handy somewhere. It was harmless enough.

Two months later came a call from the Bishop's office. Would Mr. Joiner care to serve on the diocesan Stewardship Committee?

Part Two
THE OVERVIEW

A.
The Diocese

A diocese is a gathering of congregations for the purpose of witnessing to a unified doctrine, discipline, and worship.

At some point in history, the local church, of which Joe Joiner was a member, submitted an application requesting admission into union with the Episcopal Church in that particular diocese. The application was signed by the rector, wardens, and vestrymen. They declared that it was the intention of the local church to obey and conform to the beliefs and lifestyle of that diocese. That was many years ago.

Over the years, the parish and the diocese seemed to have gone their own separate ways, and few of the parishioners cared one way or the other. Relations were pleasant enough, but recently no one made any effort to discover what that unified doctrine, discipline, and worship really meant. Everyone assumed that he or she was Episcopalian and always had been and, presumably, always would be.

The Bishop was the focal point of the life and work of the diocese. He was a priest who had been elevated through an election of his peers and lay delegates assembled in a Diocesan

Convention. His election to the episcopate was endorsed by the Standing Committees of at least a majority of dioceses throughout the Episcopal Church. He was the spiritual leader and, one hoped, the chief executive officer of his diocese. He was the symbol of Ecclesiastical Authority.[34]

The Bishop had confirmed Joe's son a year ago. He preached in a loud booming voice, he looked resplendent in his vestments, and he was very pleasant in a formal sort of way. The Bishop liked people and he was liked by them, but Joe thought he did not know him well.

On a cold and windy night in January, Joe met the Bishop for the second time. The Bishop had asked that Joe, along with nineteen others from the diocese, meet with him at the Cathedral House. The purpose of the meeting was to form a totally new *Stewardship Committee*.

It was a new committee for a new process. For the last few years the diocese had conducted its convention in the spring, at which time they voted on budgets for the following year. There were complaints about this, mostly centered around the fact that many months elapsed between the passing of the budget and its implementation. Conditions in the diocese changed too rapidly for such a delay. This year, after the necessary constitutional and canonical changes, the Diocesan Convention would be held on the first Saturday in November. The Stewardship Committee would have eight months to prepare the diocese for its first November convention.

Joe was one of ten new members (of a committee of twenty) who had never served within the diocesan organization. The Bishop asked for co-chairmen. Stacey Status volunteered. Active in the diocese for ten years, she had a reputation as a thoroughly dedicated church-person (who insisted, by the way, that she be referred to as a church-person at all times), but with no outward signs of enthusiasm. But she was a crackerjack with details. The Bishop looked around for her co-leader.

Would one of the newer members volunteer? Joe could not resist. He raised his hand. He and Stacey would serve as co-chairpersons.

An Overview

The first thing Joe said to his wife when he got home later that night was, "Well, here I go again."

"Are you sure you won't regret it?" asked Betty.

Joe was not sure, but the information he was given at the first meeting with the Bishop was too intriguing to ignore. "The issue isn't expansion," Joe continued, "it's survival. Take a look at this!"[35]

> 1. In spite of rising church income, the church's annual share in the national income began to diminish as early as 1962.
>
> 2. At the same time, local church operating expenses have been mounting more rapidly than parish income. This has been happening for a decade at least, and at an accelerating pace.
>
> 3. From 1961 until the recession year of 1970, the average benevolence allocation to diocesan and national causes went up each year more rapidly than did the amount the average parish spent on its own operations. But while benevolences drew increasing percentages of parish income, dioceses may nevertheless have been hard pressed, since diocesan expenses, including the cost of aided and mission parishes, must also be presumed to have gone up rapidly.
>
> 4. The number of parishes on the rolls began to go down after 1963. Because it can take years for churches to be closed, however, this may reflect an attrition rate than began earlier.
>
> 5. Expenditure on parish church building has declined almost

continuously, since 1961, and may have started to go down earlier. This suggests a lag in the formation of new parishes, and a failure to replace closed parishes that may have begun before 1961.

6. Church membership began to decline after 1966. Time lags in adjusting parish rolls make it probable that this membership decline may have begun several years earlier.

Joe sat back and remarked, "No wonder I saw some paint peeling from the walls in the diocesan office. Times are bad all over." Then he produced more evidence.

The church's declining share of national income: Church giving has gone down in relation to Gross National Product. Church giving has gone down as a percentage of Disposable Personal Incomes of Americans. Out of every $100.00 given to philanthropy in 1961, churches received $64.00; by 1970 this figure had gone down to $57.00. The Episcopal Church's share in this amount went from $2.58 to $1.89 in the same period.

Local church costs mount faster than income: Episcopal parish operating expenditures increased 58 percent from 1961 to 1970. The average rate of increase is in fact more than twice the rate of the Consumer Price Index.

The squeeze on building and benevolences: The amount Episcopal churches spent on capital improvements and building had declined by 1970 to 65 percent of the amount spent in 1961. The number of parishes declined from a peak of 7,343 in 1963 to 7,069 in 1970.

The diocese, caught in the middle of the parish and the national church, represented a variation on the buffer state; that is, it wanted to move independently but knew its very existence and purpose was dependent on the will of others, others equally concerned with the matter of survival.

"Joe," his wife asked, "what does this do to your pet slogan, *New Hope Awakes?*"

"My dear," Joe answered, "we will see. . . ."

All Conditions

In early February, when the Stewardship Committee met, they had some important data to discuss. The Diocesan Council, the executive arm of the diocese, had prepared a summary of statistics from the Parochial Reports, at least from the eighty percent of them that had come in since the first of the year.

The diocese was spread over half the state, and had one hundred parishes and missions serving ten thousand communicants. It's clergy numbered one hundred and twenty-five, one hundred and ten of whom were active.

Thirty percent of the churches were located in the two large cities, and they generated ten percent of the diocesan income. Twenty percent of the churches were located in the suburbs, and they generated eighty percent of the income. The remaining fifty percent of the churches were in rural areas, and they generated only ten percent of the diocesan income.

It looked as if the suburban churches were keeping the diocese alive. One might also guess that years ago it was the city churches that did it all.

"So what else is new?" Shep Shallow sat back in his chair, blew smoke from his large cigar, and continued, "A certain group of people in this diocese have always had to carry the freight."

"And who were they?" asked Joe.

"The decent, hard-working people, that's who. Look at our cities," Shep added, "it used to be you could walk through anywhere at night. Now look at it. You let certain people come in, and the decent people have no other choice than to move to the suburbs, where you have at least a chance to be safer."

Bull Brown and Carrie Careful, the two blacks on the committee, squirmed in their seats. They knew what was coming.

"Look, let's stop trying to pussy foot with each other." Biff Blocker wanted the floor. "As far as I'm concerned, it's the influx of colored and Puerto Ricans that has upset the apple cart." He turned to Bull Brown and continued. "Now, I don't mean anything rude or anything like that. It's just that your kind, well, look at the way you keep your homes and the streets. It's not fit for anyone to live in them. I don't see how *you* can."

Bull Brown got up and, folding the Council's report, put it in his back pocket. He looked at Biff and, after a pause, said, "Shove it, Mother!" With that, Bull turned and slowly left the room.

No one moved until he was gone.

Biff was livid. "See that?" he shouted. "You really can't even talk to them without them flying off the handle. No wonder things are like they are."

Carrie spoke next. "Perhaps Mr. Brown had as hard a working day as you, Mr. Blocker. It is possible that he, like you, came here to do some constructive work for this diocese, which I believe is the purpose of this committee. Am I right?"

Carrie's last question was directed at the chairperson, Charlotte, who quickly had everyone move to what she thought was another subject; namely, a surfacing of the bad things about the diocese.

It was a threnodic chorus: most of the parishes were having trouble meeting their budgets; income to the diocese was decreasing; attendance at diocesan functions had dwindled; so had membership in the Episcopal Churchwomen and Altar Guilds; too many people thought the diocesan administration was top heavy in staff; mission priests were more worried than ever about salary supplements; the diocese might have to borrow against capital to balance the current budget; very few people agreed with the programs being advocated by the Bishop; and, when asked, most parishioners did not know much about the diocese nor did they express any great desire to find out. They were too busy doing other things.

But there were good things too. There was a fine hospital with a home for the aged attached; a committee on narcotics with such a fine report on recent trends that it was published nationally; an innovative counseling service in one of the cities; a monthly newspaper which reached forty percent of the communicants; a bishop who answered his mail promptly.

The Stewardship Committee had its work cut out, and the eight months, which had looked like forever, now seemed no longer than a brace of tiny gasps. Once again Joe had to go back to his reading on the management of time.

Training Self

Joe, like any leader, had to train himself to make time management an involuntary action. It had to become part of his unconscious activity. But how? Well, in his reading he had come across a system for doing just that.[36] He asked himself a series of crucial questions.

First, what about *Intrinsic Importance*? Was the activity very important; must be done? Was it important; should be done? Was it not so important; might be useful? Or was it unimportant; could be eliminated?

Second, what about *Urgency*? Was it very urgent; must be done now? Was it urgent; should be done soon? Was it not urgent; a long-range must? Or was time not a factor?

Third, what about *Delegation*? Must it be done by Joe? Could it be delegated?

Fourth, what about *Conferences*? Who were the people Joe must see each day? Who must be seen frequently, not daily? Whom must Joe see regularly but not frequently? Next, whom

90 BEYOND PLEDGING

must he see only infrequently? Finally, what other personal contacts might be helpful?

The quicker this sorting out could become a natural activity for Joe, the more efficiently would he be able to cope with the challenges of his schedule.

It was ironic that his Rector, on the previous Sunday, preached from the writings of a seventeenth century Church leader: "God had given man a short time here upon earth, and yet upon this eternity depends: so that, for every hour of our life we must give account to the great judge of men and angels."[37] Mr. Joiner, take notice!

Two Tasks

On the evening of the following Thursday, Joe and his co-chairperson (he still thought the use of "person" was a puerile exercise) Stacey Status, met with the Bishop at the Downtown Club.

It was a pleasant evening, and they had a fine meal. By coffee and dessert, they got down to the business of the evening. The Bishop, having heard that Joe Joiner had become an avid reader of management and fund-raising studies, wanted to test something he had read, as he tried to explore the role of the Bishop in the daily operations of the diocese. The points came under the heading of *Motivating Employee Cooperation*.[38] He had prepared three copies, and he referred to the following notes:

How does one nurture a cooperative member? That was the question. The Bishop desired cooperation from those on his staff and, in a larger sense, of the diocese itself. It meant mutual trust and action. The cooperative member of the diocese, not unlike the employee in any enterprise, "tends to cooperate fully at every opportunity; he trusts the supervisor's [Bishop's] instructions and the company [diocesan] policy; and he has a favorable attitude, is well adjusted on the job [task] and generally goes along with what the supervisor [Bishop] and the company [Diocesan Convention] wish to accomplish."[39]

The Bishop went on to list the techniques that he could use to motivate this kind of cooperation:

He must provide adequate training. He must keep the people informed. He must provide dependable leadership. He must build a positive attitude. He must work for the interest of the member. He must give instructions properly. He must provide safe and favorable working conditions. He must ask questions. In other words, he must be a leader and not a boss. "Employees have to work *for* a boss, but can work *with* a leader."[40]

Joe was the first to comment. "What you said about the leader's role can be said for the diocese itself."

"Precisely," the Bishop answered. "The diocese has a leadership role: to provide adequate training, keep the people informed, provide dependable leadership, and so on."

"This surely gives us a good starting point, doesn't it?" Stacey made notes as she spoke. "We can build a program and budget around this outline. It could be the basis of the fund-raising campaign between now and the convention. We just have to make the obvious adjustments from employer-employee relationships to diocesan-parochial relationships."

"Okay," Joe added, "let's see what we have. The diocese must develop and get support for its program and budget. At the same time, the parish must do the same."

"Right," the Bishop added, "but usually the diocese seems to go one way and the local church another."

Out of this conversation, which lasted another hour, the three of them decided that their diocese had two tasks: *first, to develop a program and budget for those activities best done by the diocese rather than the individual church unit; and, second, to assist the local church to do its own work.*

"I have a slogan for the campaign." Stacey was excited. "Let's call it Operation Cooperation."

Joe could tell from the Bishop's facial expression that both men thought the slogan had a corny ring to it, but this might not be the time to argue about it one way or the other. It was worth thinking about, as was the details as discussed.

When they were ready to call it a night, and left the club, the Bishop offered them a ride, but Joe wanted to stop off at Bull Brown's apartment. It was not far from the club.

Bull Brown

Joe Joiner had never been in the part of the city where the Browns had an apartment. It was a slum. Dark and dingy. The apartment house was one of those projects designed by the architectural firms that usually specialized in prisons. It was dark at this hour of the evening and Joe was apprehensive as he walked into the lobby.

Two black youths, standing in the lobby, stopped speaking when Joe walked to the letterboxes in the badly lit lobby. They watched as Joe searched the nameplates for B. Brown. Many of the names were missing, but he finally found it and pushed the buzzer. He walked to the main door, waiting for the lock to be released. The two youths were enjoying themselves. Finally, one of the youths spoke.

"Hey, Whitey, what makes you think that lock works?"

"Yeah," the other youth added, "do you think we're afraid of spooks in the night?"

The two youths laughed loudly, and Joe opened the door with the broken lock, and, avoiding the elevator took the stairs two at a time.

Bull Brown was surprised to see Joe Joiner, but he welcomed him into his four rooms and introduced Joe to his wife and four sons.

When he and Bull were alone in the kitchen, Joe wanted to apologize for the remarks passed at the first meeting. Mr. Brown thought it was unnecessary to apologize.

"As the man says," Bull said with a smile, "it takes all kinds. All sorts and conditions." The subject changed. "My guess is that you've never been to this part of town." Joe had not. "You're not alone. The Diocesan Council hasn't been here either."

They searched for understanding. Bull had trouble with the hubris in Biff's and Shep's statements. These men were presumptuous to think they understood the subtleties of life in the ghetto, in this unique corner of the diocese. Bull Brown, moreover, conceded that he knew little of their environment too, and of Joe's for that matter. Joe also admitted his ignorance of the varieties of situations in the diocese. He did not understand the full dimensions of his own parish, how could he possibly be expected to know the diocese? Bull Brown knew his own parish all too well, it was all slum.

The problem, as these men saw it, was a failure to identify what the diocese really was. It was neither slum nor suburb, neither Bull Brown nor Shep Shallow. It was both. It was something different from the official definition of a diocese; indeed, it was a complex scattering of people who, in some part, had a highly individualized concept of purpose and mission which only occasionally presented itself as a unified voice and action. Hopefully, these men would have the sense to keep this in mind.

As It Was

The second meeting of the Stewardship Committee lasted for most of a Saturday in late February. Joe presided. The twenty members plus the Bishop and ten of his Diocesan Council were present. The thirty-one of them had full use of the Cathedral House, which meant that they could meet, and eat the catered lunch, in the same place. It was a full working day.

Joe wanted them to face the realities of the diocese. Stacey had mimeographed the list of what was good and bad about the diocese, as revealed in the previous meeting. They studied this list. Joe noticed that the expressions on the faces of some of the council members suggested trouble ahead. He was right. The vice president of the council, a distinguished looking clergyman from one of the largest parishes in the diocese, felt obligated for the sake of this committee to emphasize that the diocese and its beloved Bishop were doing a first-class job and it would be misleading if not cruel to suggest otherwise, as the list suggested. Next Stacey Status, in an impassioned speech that lasted fifteen minutes, made certain the Bishop and clergy knew they were loved and cherished for the outstanding job they were doing for the sake of God's mission.

Joe held his temper. "Ladies and gentlemen," he said, "I do not think it necessary to defend our people and diocese. We have a lot of good going for us. On the other hand, life here can be better. We're winning some, and losing some. The purpose of this committee is to assist the diocese in winning more than losing. Is what I am saying reasonable?"

The distinguished clergyman did not think it was reasonable. "Even to suggest that we are losing some, as you say, can be picked up in the papers and used in the worst possible way." He looked around and received, as if on cue, reserved but supportive nods from the members of his council. "The point, Mr. Joiner, is that those of us who have dedicated our life's work for the spread of His Kingdom cannot and should not countenance, er . . ." He had not used the word he wanted and, in trying to find it, forgot what he was going to say.

The Bishop took the opportunity of this pause to remind the others that the church, in its priestly sense, had a dual role to perform. "We are required" he said, "to administer the sacraments, and also, to protect them. I wonder if we do not err by putting too much emphasis on protecting them; thereby becoming guilty of such an exclusivity that we become detached from the very people we are called upon to serve."

This was not where Joe expected the meeting to go, but he was delighted, nevertheless. The Bishop had said what had to be said. "And, Bishop," Joe said, "when we consider that God calls for a priesthood of all believers, it is our bounden duty to administer and to protect all that the church possesses." Joe surprised himself at his words.

"Yes indeed," the Bishop responded.

As We Want It

By the luncheon break each committee member felt relaxed enough to admit that the diocese was not perfect, but it was far from rotten.

During the afternoon, those who had not eaten too much of the macaroni and cheese (Joe reminded himself to order only light lunches for future all-day meetings) focused on an identity question. They considered a working paper Joe and Stacey ordered from a group known as SALT Associates. (They had made copies for each member of the group.)[41]

The paper addressed itself to the gap between the identity

and mission of a group, as that group wants it to be and as it really is. To find the identity of a diocese, for instance, requires an understanding of its origins, its values and traditions, its accomplishments, its present intentions. Then the questions must be posed: Where will the diocese go under its present momentum, without new influences? Are goals being actively set or merely resulting from inertia?[42] A serious approach to such queries will clarify the concept of mission—actual and potential—of the diocese.

The Stewardship Committee and the Diocesan Council agreed to additional meetings to work on a four-part study suggested in this working paper.[43]

First, they studied the organization from three viewpoints: (a) the elements of tradition, or "genesis" that the diocese might consider important right now; (b) its present structure and activities; (c) its future direction as suggested by its present momentum, which then summarized in a five-year forecast.

Second, they analyzed (a), (b), and (c). These were the hard data. Using no other data, they each completed the statement: This diocese is in the business of _____? Then sentences reflected what each had learned from the data, and those data alone. They discussed the various answers in order that they might reach a consensus.

Third, each answered the same question but from a different point of view, That is, now each told what he or she wanted the diocese to stand for; and what each wanted the publicity to express. Again the statement: This diocese is in the business of _____? Once again, they reached for a consensus.

Fourth, they compared their answers arrived at in steps 2 and 3. The gap between the statements in step 2 and step 3 represented the gap between identity and mission as it actually existed and as they wanted it to be. The research and planning which was to follow demanded that the participants hold in tension the two extremes: *what they wanted it to be* versus *what it really was.* Why? To bridge the gap between the two.

This four-part exercise pinpointed many realities of diocesan activities. For instance, the Stewardship Committee had a good issue in the narcotics program, but, as Bull Brown and others told them, the study that received such favorable notice in the church nationally was, in reality, too esoteric and sophisticated for the very people it was attempting to reach in this diocese. Teenagers wanted a practical alternative to a life of pain and horror, not a narcotics study replete with diagrams charting interrelations between government and individual.

Regional Meetings

Obviously the people of the diocese must be heard. And so the Stewardship Committee planned a series of regional meetings.

Successful meetings depended, first, upon adequate publicity. One month before the schedule meetings *written* notices were sent to each parish and to each newspaper in the diocese. Ten days before the meeting dates, *direct, informal* contact was made with key people by telephone. The Bishop phoned each clergyman in the diocese and committee members telephoned each Senior Warden. Both the written and verbal communications contained essentially the same information i.e.: *What*: a meeting was to be held for the purpose of gathering information preparatory to building a diocesan program and budget for the next year, to be presented at this year's Diocesan Convention. *When*: on such-and-such day between the hours of such-and-such. *Where*: at a specified place. *Who*: to be led by members of the Stewardship Committee, and with representatives from each local church present. *Why*: it was crucial to make sure the proposed program and budget reflected the real needs in the diocese.

Stacey's slogan *Operation Cooperation* was used. And, sure enough, by the time the meetings were held people were referring to the OC. This annoyed Joe. It was so easy to remember the letters and forget what they stood for. His rector said this had been one of the dangers of the famous MRI program of a few years back. People got so used to saying MRI that they forgot it stood for Mutual Responsibility and Interdependence in the Body of Christ. The Body of Christ got chopped off somewhere between this diocese and that missionary district. Joe said nothing, however, but he made certain that he always used the full expression, Operation Cooperation.

The Stewardship Committee sought maximum involvement on the part of the participants in the regional meetings, which in turn would (one hoped) foster maximum involvement on the parish level in diocesan programs. Joe and his committee reviewed two basic arguments for such group procedures: (1) *"Valuable data needed in a solution of a local problem are buried in the experiences of the local people, data that can be uncovered through the proper use of group procedures."* (2) *"When people are involved in the development of plans, they are more willing and ready to give time and effort to seeing the plans carried through."*[44]

And so when the regional meetings were held, the Stewardship Committee listened and, for the most part, remained silent. This was the time to gather data.

The meetings were kept informal, with a spirit of openness. Participants (from five to ten persons with varying ages and outlook at any one regional meeting) sat in a circle or around a table as a member of the Stewardship Committee described some phase of the diocesan program and budget as objectively as possible. Bull Brown, for example, described the work of the women's guilds. A few weeks earlier, Bull knew nothing about this work and had to gather the necessary information, had to learn before he was called upon to explain. It was hoped

THE OVERVIEW 99

that, in doing it this way, the speaker would provide a more objective view than, in the case of women's guilds, for instance, the president of a guild might. Bull could explain what he knew about the work, without defending or promoting it.

Generally, this scheme worked and the participants responded to what was essentially a fair, unbiased presentation. The committee collected voluminous data.

Community

Who was pushing the diocese for special programs? What secular groups wanted support from the religious entities such as the diocese? Did secular groups with no allegiance to the particular faith have any right to ask the diocese for support? Wasn't the primary obligation of the diocese to propagate the faith?

Puzzling questions like these occupied the Stewardship Committee at its next meeting. Bull Brown was adamant. "Who cares if these brothers and sisters recite our creeds or not," he said. "They're hurting and we have to help them."

Shep Shallow responded, "Charity starts at home."

"I always worry about charity starting at home," Joe Joiner added. "When we try to satisfy all our demands at home, we seldom end up satisfied. I, for instance, would have tennis equipment coming out of my ears. And all of it purchased under the guise of emergency necessities for health and breath."

"Then you need controls," said Biff Blocker. "Discipline." Turning to Bull Brown he added, "Exactly what this country needs more of."

"Friends?" Stacey Status, who was presiding over the meeting, had the floor. "We can't give away what we don't have, but, on the other hand, we can find out what non-diocesan groups want. Right?"

But which groups did one approach, and by what tactics? Nearly everyone present had his own favorite group. The Bishop and other key clergy sat on a number of community boards and agencies. These, naturally enough, emerged near the top of the list.

Rodney Ram, a young man in his early twenties, and until now silent, spoke up. "Are we only going to hear from the darling pets of the French Court?"

"I beg your pardon?" asked an indignant Archdeacon, his eyebrows nearly disappearing under his finely combed gray hair.

"Oh, you know what I'm talking about," answered Rodney. "There are some groups that are favorites and there are others that never get their story told to us or anyone else. That's the way things are. For years, the diocese has played along with a few, and let the others starve to death."

"We can't do everything," Stacey reminded him.

"Look," continued Rodney, "I'm the first to admit that. It's just that we have no real, open system for letting new groups state their case to us."

Shep Shallow broke in. "We have more than we can handle as it is. I agree with Stacey Status, we can't do everything."

"Hear, hear!" the Archdeacon agreed.

Joe Joiner added, "If we are going to be true to our system of decision making, then we have to hear from all sources, those unfamiliar ones as well as the favorites of what Rodney calls the French Court." There were some mumbles, but no one objected to the fairness of inclusivity.

Carrie Careful wanted to say something: "It just occurred to me that we always assume that the only thing these outside organizations want from us is money."

"What else?" Biff was enjoying himself. "Do you think they want us to hold their hands without our putting a few dollars in them first?"

"Perhaps," Carrie retorted, getting everyone's attention. She went on. "These groups might want from us moral support—maybe all they want is our understanding and acceptance of what they are saying and what they are trying to do. Why do we always think someone is hitting us for money? Is this all the church has to offer?"

The Bishop asked Carrie what she thought the diocese could offer these groups.

"Love, acceptance, and a sense of friendship in a not too friendly society," was Carrie's answer. "And perhaps a feeling of spirituality about their process. Just perhaps."

"Just a lot of bunk," added Biff.

"Then," concluded Carrie, "it's time we took the trouble to find out."

"It seems to me," Joe said, "the diocese should offer what only it can offer. And that is a spiritual sense about life. It's our faith that makes us unique. Why don't we look for ways to distribute that."

Joe's comment triggered a series of supportive statements by almost all the committee. While others were speaking, Joe could not help thinking to himself that he had come a long way from the mere joiner who preferred to slip into the rear pew. He thought how Betty would get a kick out of having a religious fanatic in the home. Joe felt good about what he was doing and saying.

Stacey Status led everyone through a discussion on ways the committee could reach all the secular groups in the diocese.

The Stewardship Committee spent six weeks compiling a list of agencies, a task that was accomplished through a variety of methods. Rectors and vicars were consulted. Local telephone books were perused. Key laypersons were requested to furnish names of secular groups. Political leaders of all parties were contacted. By the end of the six weeks, the list was overwhelming.

Shep Shallow and Bull Brown then organized the list into categories for easy reference; that is, agencies dealing with health services, groups working in specific social action areas, etc. This task of refinement and simplification entailed three more weeks of work and thirty arguments about interpretation of purpose.

By early May the committee had a list of forty agencies divided into four general categories, of which they selected one, Drugs and Alcohol, for special diocesan help.

Tasks

In the meanwhile, requests for continuing and new programs were coming in from the staff and volunteer personnel of the diocese. By mid-May, this information was assembled and the Finance Committee had prepared the initial budget request.[45] (See Table 6.)

The proposal/budget page was divided into three sections. The *first* offered a brief description of the Program Task to be supported. It started its task as succinctly as possible. (A task had been defined as specific and measurable targets or projects.)

The *second* section consisted of three figures: *(a)* what was actually disbursed the previous year; *(b)* what was budgeted for the current year, since it was too early to give current disbursements; and *(c)* what was being proposed, at this stage of the process, for the next year.

Using a scale of 1 (highest) to 5 (lowest), the *third* section summarized priority ratings of each task from the point of view of (a) the Diocesan Council, including staff recommendations, (b) local church, (c) Stewardship Committee. At this stage columns *(b)* and *(c)* were still blank. Two copies of this

Table 6
DIOCESAN BUDGET REQUEST

Program*	Financial Support**			Priorities***		
	Actuals Previous Year	Budget Current Year	Proposed Next Year	Diocesan Council Bishop and Staff	The Church Units	The Stewardship Committee
A brief description of the program	$	$	$	1 to 5	1 to 5	1 to 5

* Program: Is is necessary to describe the specific program as objectively as possible.
** Financial Support: Normally, it is impossible to show the actual budget for the current year.
*** Priorities: The Bishop and Staff place their priorities in concert with the executive arm of the diocese, the Council. The priorities from the Church Units offer the second point of view. The third, and, in some cases, the most distant viewpoint, comes from the Stewardship Committee, who can remain removed. The clergy and delegates to convention will then make the final decision concerning priorities and financial support.

initial proposal were sent to each parish and mission, with a covering letter explaining the material and asking that each parish fill in column *(b)* and return one copy of the page to the Stewardship Committee before June 10. The Stewardship Committee would then analyze the information and re-submit its final proposal budget program and budget during the second week of September.

Summer

By the end of June, more than seventy percent of the churches had returned their materials as requested. Fortunately the committee had given itself lead time. The complaints were strident: the committee was charged by some with failing to hear the people at the regional meetings. Others said it was not radical enough, not liberal enough, not conservative enough, just a bunch of company men, with the same old self-serving interests, the whole thing a waste of paper and postage. Not everyone complained, but enough had.

Joe and Stacey, the co-chairpersons, whose signatures had been on the covering letter that went out with the proposal, were dismayed. They brought the matter before the committee for discussion, from which the following points emerged:

Cost controls. Inflation was hurting everyone, and there had been a hope that the diocesan budget would be cut no matter what programs were affected. If the diocese was not ready to take the lead, well, who was?

Personnel. There was growing disenchantment with many staff people, and the critics wanted them out rather than supply them with more money. Eliminate the man, the argument went, and you save the money for something else. For some, to cut the budget, meant to show their real anger for the Bishop in a real but safe manner.

The process. The idea that a Stewardship Committee, other than the Diocesan Council, was now operating and following a new process was more upsetting than the Bishop had realized. Many people liked the way things were done. Well, it wasn't that they liked the old ways, but they were familiar with them, and they were not in the mood to judge new ones.

The mailing. It looked too pat, too fancy, too final. Yes, it was mimeographed and not printed but, still, it had a finality about it which turned people off. There were complaints by some about misspelled names. A few, unfortunately, never received their copies.

Integrity. The Stewardship Committee had requested a decrease in diocesan support for the national church program, but, at the same time requested an increase for diocesan projects. Why shouldn't the local congregation take a similar attitude, and decrease its pledge to the diocese while increasing the budget for local uses?

Timing. People were rushed into a new process, and if they were unable to make the regional meeting, they were out of luck; their voice was not heard. Moreover, there were still many who did not like the idea of changing the date of the convention no matter how successful it might be in other dioceses. Furthermore, who wanted to think about next year's program and budget in June when the local church was winding down for the summer of the current year?

The committee thought that many of these judgments were unreasonable, but in no case did Joe Joiner allow the members to dismiss them disdainfully. They were important as revealing the attitudes of parish members, and they would be kept in mind.

Review

The summer would be spent tabulating column *(b)* as submitted by the local church units, preparatory to the Stewardship Committee's final report to be mailed early in September.

Joe Joiner wrote a memo to the committee members, with copies to the Bishop, staff, and Diocesan Council, stating the timetable and other administrative details. He also reviewed some of the concepts that had seemed so vital to them as they began their work a few months before.

The Bishop, Joe reminded them, felt that the committee had two tasks for this year: first, to develop a program and budget for those things best done by the diocese rather than the individual church unit; and second, to assist the local church to do its own work. So far, they had not done much about the second task and some were already feeling that, had the second objective preceded the first, many of the harsh criticisms might have been avoided. It was something to think about for the future.

Joe also reminded them of their earlier consensus on group procedures, namely: "Valuable data needed in a solution of a local problem are buried in the experiences of the local people, data that can be uncovered through the proper use of group procedures. And when people are involved in the development of plans, they are more willing and ready to give time and effort to seeing the plans carried through."

In reviewing these basics for the committee, Joe was also reminding himself of essentials as a leader. Too often, he had found, it was easy to read a great idea, use it once or twice, and then put it away under the impression that it had become part of the process. Sometimes it had become a part of the process, but often it was lost and forgotten. In writing this to others, Joe was reminding himself of what they were trying to do and why, and how they were attempting to go about it.

Leadership

As Joe Joiner became more sure of himself and the committee members, and was able to delegate more work and authority to others, he was able to relax more. He could even concentrate on his tennis game.

One afternoon on the courts, however, he made a slip of the tongue. It was during a break in a doubles match with his wife and their neighbors, when Joe was asked how he felt his church work was progressing.

"Well," Joe answered, "so far so good. There are problems, but my committee has come a long way."

"Whose committee?" asked his neighbor.

"Mine," said Joe. Then he laughed, as did his wife, Betty. They had been through this before. "You see," Joe explained, "I have this king-of-the-mountain fixation, and, at times, I call it my personal committee."

Later that night, when Joe and his wife discussed this particular ingredient of leadership, Betty made an analogy to their own marriage. "I suppose it can be said that I am your wife and you are my husband, because we each will this to be so."

"Our role," added Joe, "is mutually dependent. Which means, of course, that the I am a leader of the committee as long as—"

"—as long as the committee wills it," Betty finished. "Kind of humbling, isn't it?"

"Isn't it?" concluded Joe. He reached for his notebook, which by now was full of quotations from his readings. He found what he wanted. "Listen to this," and he read, " 'Leadership is a function of the group; a group confers leadership on a member when that member offers what the group wants.' "[46]

"And I thought I had an original idea," responded Betty with a twinkle in her eye.

Joe reached over and kissed his wife. "Do you realize," he said, "that I never would have been able to get involved in this Episcopal Church if it hadn't been the fact that you made it possible for me to do so." She smiled. Then the two of them looked at all the papers he had to go through before the next meeting of the Stewardship Committee, and they laughed. "Which is," he concluded, "a mixed blessing, isn't it?"

PRECONVENTION

The first week in September came too soon for the Stewardship Committee. Gathering a quorum together for summer meetings had proved well-nigh impossible. Joe and Stacey agreed that, in the event of future committees, they would hope for fewer members.

Joe and Stacey called a meeting for the first Friday following Labor Day, determined to do business whoever attended. Luckily, they had a quorum. Tish Tepid, showing more interest than she had a few months before, took charge and led them through the analysis of the column *(b)*, that is, the responses from the local church units.

Priorities

Shep Shallow wanted to make a change in the process. It occurred to him that the diocese had put its faith in the

Stewardship Committee, criticisms notwithstanding, and it was their duty to submit a proposal for program and budget exclusive of the priorities from either the church units or the Diocesan Council.

Joe thought this was the silliest thing he had ever heard, but he was getting smart enough to hold his tongue. A couple of others in the meeting who felt as Joe did were more vocal.

Tish asked Shep to give his reason. Shep tried to say something about three columns cluttering the page the sole job of the Stewardship Committee should be to gather information and then come in with its recommendation. Shep might have had a good point or two, but no one in the room wanted to bother with him.

Joe, remembering what had happened in a parish meeting when Curt Conflict alienated the group, changed the tack in the hope of calming the process. He reminded them of what they had agreed to earlier concerning priorities. *Priorities*, simply put, were orders of preference put into play by individuals working alone or with others. Everyone had priorities of some kind, and the danger came when a basic fact was forgotten: when you add something you usually have to be ready to take away something else. Any exercise to determine priorities was like doing the marketing. It was one thing to want lots more ice cream next week, but if the budget remained the same, what could be given up, cheese or laundry? What if, however, the budget increased? Would fifty percent of the increase be given to ice cream, twenty-five percent to cheese, and the rest to laundry? And if the budget decreased? Was it to be iced-milk instead of the creamier dessert? Would it be a tiny bit of Camembert instead of a hunk of Velveeta? What had to be relinquished for the sake of gaining something else? Giving was related to getting.

The committee decided that, for purposes of integrity the final proposal for program and budget would emphasize the word "proposal." The covering letter stated that it would be the decision of the Diocesan Convention to make the final judgment about everything proposed. The letter went on to say that the Stewardship Committee would present the three columns for reference, and that they would say something about how they judged priorities in view of these various responses.

The mailing went to all clergy and delegates to the convention. It was urged that each Vestry or Executive Committee should make this proposal part of their own agenda, preferably before they set in motion their own Every Member Canvass. This way, parochial and diocesan effort could perhaps be seen as one. The members of the Stewardship Committee were pleased that they had done their job and had done it with enough lead time for the parishes to discuss the details.

Later, on the telephone, Joe and Stacey compared notes. Joe had succeeded in making a point about priorities, but he had failed to deal with Shep Shallow's argument or with Shep's relationship to the committee.

But what about Shep Shallow's argument and his relationship to the committee? Shep was feeling less a part of things. If this continued, Shep would feel less interested and his performance would show it. Shep had not been given enough to do, he felt out of things. Joe and Stacey, when they discussed this on the phone, did not want to give Shep an extra job just to get him involved, that was never an intelligent way of getting participation. They would keep the problem in mind.

Once again, Joe recalled the three basics of group work. First, there was a need to accomplish the goal. Second, there was a need to maintain the integrity of the group itself. Third, and this is where they were failing with Shep Shallow, there was a need to guarantee that the individual would sense a genuine feeling of purpose and participation.

Lobbies

The Archdeacon called Joe the following week. He had requested and received the Bishop's endorsement—which he referred to as a blessing—to hold a series of regional meetings before the Convention.

"Why?" asked Joe.

"For the purpose of saving our programs, that's why!" The Archdeacon did not give details but it was not difficult for Joe to sense that the senior priest's nose was out of joint. For what reason, though, Joe could not tell.

For years, the Diocesan Council had sat with the staff, and together they decided on the program and budget. The Bishop knew that this system was self-perpetuating in that the staff were judging their own performance and, as long as they were in that position, they would spend most of their time justifying their job by seeking acceptance. The Bishop was determined to change this system, and that was why he had called for a totally new and independent Stewardship Committee.

Joe and Stacey met with the Bishop to find out why he had endorsed this procedure. The Bishop explained that another hearing could very well involve many more people, and the more people discussing this proposal the better. Second, the Bishop felt that he would rather have the arguments for and against the program and budget take place in small meetings, before rather than during the convention itself. Joe and Stacey had no argument with these reasons.

The convention, the Bishop continued, was a bore to many people and attendance had fallen in the last few years. One of the complaints had been lengthy debates over minutiae, which included, for some, program details. The Bishop was pleased that the Stewardship Committee had opened up the process in general.

"And if that is so," the Bishop concluded, "well, let us consider the Diocesan Council meetings an important part of the whole process."

The hearings were more than the Archdeacon had bargained for. Getting the delegates to come to another meeting right before the convention, especially to hear a series of impassioned pleas for continuing this or that pet program, backfired. Word got around and, by the time the third meeting, less than five percent of the delegates attended.

"It served them right," was Joe's impromptu assessment to the committee members, since he was convinced their failure justified his own procedure.

Carrie Careful cautioned Joe and others not to be so hasty. "What we failed to do," she said, "was to bring them into the process right at the beginning. I wonder how we would have felt suddenly being sidestepped after so many years of running things our own way? Perhaps," she continued, "they were merely filling a void left by poor management in the past."

"Neat point," admitted Joe. "Fighting for positions of power rather than getting a job done."

Bull Brown added, "Fighting for power positions is what it's all about . . . eh, Biff?"

Biff Blocker was not listening to what Bull said, and Bull did not bother repeating it.

The Mailing

The Stewardship Committee took upon itself to make a change from the initial proposal for program and budget before sending it out to the clergy and delegates to the Diocesan Convention. They varied the wording of the text so that it reflected more closely what each department was trying to say. The regional meetings had been helpful here. There was always a difference between what someone wrote formally about his particular work and what he said about it in a more informal and verbal setting.

Rodney Ram and Stacey Status did the rewriting, and it was a good choice because each held the reins on the other. It took them a little longer to complete the text, but the result was lean copy saying exactly what had to be said; more facts than flourishes.

The committee then filled in their column *(c)* with what they believed were reasonable recommendations in view of what they had learned from the total process. In most cases the recommendations were different from those of the column *(a)* (Diocesan Council and staff), and column *(b)* (the local church units).

Carrie Careful made certain the diocesan mailing list was accurate by discreetly appearing at the diocesan office on four consecutive afternoons, under the pretense of checking her own list against that of the diocese. Whenever she found a mistake, and she found many, she remained silent but made two entries. She meant to keep peace in the administrative family.

The covering letter, over Stacey and Joe's signatures, neither justified the recommendations or the process nor mentioned the extra meetings of the Diocesan Council. The committee did not want to judge or sell anything.

Finally the mailing went to all the clergy and delegates— the most thorough presentation of facts and figures ever attempted in the diocese.

Contacts

Joe had one last thought. The Bishop had complained about the lack of interest at the convention and the small attendance.

"I have an idea!" exclaimed Rodney Ram. What he had in mind was that each member of the Stewardship Committee take one or two particular programs or major areas of concern, such as Christian Education, Narcotics, or Women's Guilds, and be responsible for contacting those parish members who might have a special interest in the specific program and budget.

"This way," Rodney continued "we might be able to personalize the specific work with that person most keenly interested, and, therefore, the one who will take the most care to be on hand to see what is done to his or her pet project. We could create lots of little lobby groups scurrying here and there like little mice on the convention floor."

Shep Shallow's mind was elsewhere, and unfortunately his comment was, "What was that about mice?"

Rodney let him have it. "Why Shep, old friend, we are going to create a department of rodent control, perhaps to be used as living pets for our Sunday schools. You know, we could have the kids make little costumes and such—"

"Okay, friends," Joe interjected, "let's not allow your good point to chase after some irrelevant piece of cheese, okay?" It was the best Joe could come up with at the moment, and since Rodney laughed (with Joe or at him?) it did not matter so long as Rodney got off Shep's back and returned to the essential point. Joe continued. "It seems to me that this is a good idea, and as long as we don't come across as advocates for this or that program we'll provide a service."

"Our telephoning," Carrie added, "could emphasize the fact

we were calling to answer any questions about the report, and if we stated their particular case with clarity, we surely would demonstrate that we all had a stake in the process."

This procedure of calling key people in the diocese was adopted, and Rodney quickly split the one list into several, so that each member would have one. He failed, however, to give Shep Shallow a list, a snub which Shep seemed to understand all too well, but to which he made no response.

The committee was ahead of schedule so it was decided to call a special meeting to hear a preliminary report on some of the ideas they might use to formulate a service to the members of the diocese following the convention. It appeared that the committee was functioning very well and all seemed happy and content; all except Shep Shallow.

DEFERRED GIVING

The regional hearing, reinforced by the Diocesan Council meeting, had revealed a need for information-sharing regarding the various ways in which a person or organization could contribute to the work of the church. This information would be supplied to the local church units following the convention, but the committee heard the preliminary report now so they might have these data in the back of their minds during the convention; not necessarily so they could pop up on the floor of the convention with quick, superficial answers but so they might be better able to relate their information to the needs as expressed by the delegates.

The Stewardship Committee heard reports about Foundations and Deferred Giving.

Foundations were legally organized methods for the purposeful distribution of money, normally to projects about to begin rather than to people looking for a continuation of an uncertain salary. Of the more than twenty-five thousand private Foundations, many give money to church-related projects. Thumbing through a directory of foundations will usually reveal which of the Foundations are attracted to religious efforts.

Foundations hire executives who screen proposals; therefore, the idea must be sold to them first of all. The following questions must be asked as the proposal is being developed:[47]

> Why is the project being proposed? What is the need? Is the need real or something manufactured to get some money? Are the objectives of the project realistic in terms of the need? Will it do what is needed?
> How are these objectives going to be met? Are the methods and techniques sound, and is the timetable reasonable?
> Will there be a proper mechanism for the honest evaluation of the results of the project? Who will evaluate?
> What facilities and personnel will be needed to accomplish the objectives of the project?
> When the grant period runs out, what plans are there for continuing the project?
> How much will the project cost? What monies have been spent already, and why?

The proposal can be put into writing and submitted too soon, a common error. A personal contact with an executive or trustee of the Foundation, is important for a number of reasons, not the least of which is the opportunity it provides to develop the proposal with the Foundation itself. It becomes a shared opportunity for mutual service. Only about ten percent of philanthropy comes from Foundations, but, to say the least, that represents a substantial amount of money. Foundations need to give a percentage of their money away; it is only natural that church-related groups can be proper recipients for the right reasons.

The preliminary report on Deferred Giving was more complicated than the Stewardship Committee had anticipated. When contributions are postponed until some future date, the legal details become complex, and are usually beyond the expertise of local church units. These methods of giving, therefore, were usually ignored as being too sophisticated. But, complicated or not, they were something to consider.

Deferred giving dealt with monies and assets pledged or assigned to be delivered at a later date. These could be in the form of insurance, annuities, memorials, and wills.[48]

Take Carrie Careful's giving, for example. She normally gave three hundred dollars per annum to her parish. This was given in monthly donations; she could not afford to give this amount in one lump sum. She was in her forties and expected to stay in the same parish for the rest of her life. The parish, therefore, could expect to receive this money as long as she lived.

What tangible gift could the parish expect to receive after Carrie's death? Under normal circumstances, nothing. But what if Carrie made it possible for the parish to receive a fixed sum per year now *and* money after her death?

Insurance was one way to make this gift possible. Making the parish the beneficiary of an insurance policy might appeal to Carrie for two reasons. First of all, the annual premiums would be more manageable than, say, a large donation right now. Second, because the parish was to receive the principal of the policy, the annual premiums would be tax-deductible. The parish, moreover, would be able to borrow against the policy during these years. The fact that the parish might borrow against this policy added to its attractiveness.

In most cases, as people got older their insurance needs diminished. But Carrie wanted to protect an indigent brother. She could make the brother the primary beneficiary with the parish, as second beneficiary, receiving the rest.

Tish Tepid, more wealthy than Carrie, could consider an

annuity agreement as her way of making a substantial contribution to her parish.

Tish, through her lawyer, could donate a house and acreage to the parish. The gift would be the property of the parish, and the parish would maintain it. The donor would receive a sum of money for this maintenance as agreed upon and would also receive a tax deduction on a continuing basis. Upon Tish's death the property would remain as part of the assets of the parish.

There are variations on this form of giving. *Life Income Contract* whereby "the donor turns over money or property to the church which agrees to pay him for life a percentage return on that amount equal to the percentage earned by its endowment fund." *Taxfree Trust*, whereby the "donor transfers money or property to a trust to invest the funds in tax-exempt bonds." *Charitable Remainder Trust*, whereby the "donor transfers money or property to a trustee to hold the property, invest the same, and pay the income of the trust to the donor himself, his wife, or children," with the remainder eventually going back to the church.[49]

"Wait a minute," said Bull Brown. "Do you think my people are going to understand this?"

"No better than mine," Joe answered, "unless we make sure the language and the examples are simple. Let's get together and see what we can come up with, okay?"

"Okay," Bull said.

Joe, still self-conscious about his relationship to Bull Brown, made a note in his folder to call Bull tomorrow. That was one contact he did not want to forget.

Memorials was the next item in the preliminary report on Deferred Giving. This was a common method of giving in churches. People like to be identified with a gift such as a pulpit, window, or chalice. Too often, however, the donor fails to provide funds for the proper maintenance of the gift, and this is frequently the fault of the church for not reminding the donor at the time of the gift.

Bull expressed the hope that they could encourage more people to set up programs as memorials, real live, on-going programs that kept people alive and not just for dead memorials like marble plaques on the walls.

"Those marble plaques," Biff Blocker reminded him, "represented contributions that kept many an inner-city parish open, don't you forget that."

"Kept mausoleums open, you mean!"

"Yeah, that's right," Biff lashed out at him. "Big fancy places that are not appreciated by the people who presently use them."

"Hey, friends," Joe said hurriedly, "the report on Brotherly Love will be given next week." Bull Brown smiled. Biff Blocker did not. Joe did not care one way or the other. He was getting tired.

Carrie wanted to finish the report with a few comments about *wills*. The legal necessity for wills was unquestioned; perhaps it was time to consider its theological place. Could this committee be so bold as to preach the need for a Christian will? What points would they make? Carrie gave four reasons she had picked up in her own research.[50]

A Christian will, first, witnessed to the testator's belief in God, and he might even begin it with the words, "In the name of God, Amen," and proceed from there. Second, a Christian's will made provision for people and organizations as they related to the wholeness of God's creation itself and not merely for a single family or parochial interest. Third, a Christian's will set forth the details of the funeral and disposal of the body. Fourth, a Christian's will acknowledged that life in God's creation is continuous, and proper provisions were to be made to help. A Christian's will, therefore, was more than a legal document, it was a testimony of one's faith and practice in the world.

"Good stuff," exclaimed Rodney Ram. "We'll force the faith right down into their bank accounts."

His comment might have been meant good-naturedly, but Joe noticed that some of the committee squirmed in their seats. Shep Shallow got up from his chair and walked to the door, only to be stopped by Stacey Status.

"May I have the floor?" she asked. Shep returned to his chair, and she continued. "Mr. Ram, I resent your insinuation that—"

"Hey," Rodney interrupted, "where's your sense of humor? Can't we have any fun among ourselves?"

"If I may continue." Stacey stood tall and firm as she brushed an imaginary hair from her eyes, which focused away from Rodney. "Once anyone in the diocese suspects we are being less than serious about our work, our credibility will be lost forever."

"Forever?" taunted Rodney. "Isn't that a little bit too dramatic?"

Shep came to her defense. "Why don't you let the woman finish?" Rodney held up his hands, and sat back in his chair.

The point Stacey Status made was that any portion of fund raising in churches was always suspect by a great many people who thought that was all the church ever did. To joke about it, no matter how lightly, could be misinterpreted.

Rodney protested. "What, are we getting too staid to see any humor anymore? We're like a bunch of old fogeys."

Stacey turned red, and flicked more invisible hairs from the front of her face. Shep Shallow, again on his feet, wanted to know when the meeting would be over—he had a very busy day coming up.

Tish hurriedly summarized the points reached in the reports about Deferred Giving, the subject matter for the evening, and reminded everyone that the examples given were to be kept in mind while they listened to people speak at the convention next month. "Some new program," she said, "might best be served through deferred giving, and it might be our job to assist that in happening." No one argued the point, especially in view of the late hour. They adjourned until they would meet, in another role, at the convention.

COFFEE BREAK

On the evening before the Diocesan Convention, the Joe Joiners invited the Rector and his wife to their home for what they hoped would be a relaxing evening, with the added promise that they would not talk shop. That was until Joe opened his mail to find a terse note from Shep Shallow. Mr. Shallow was sorry but he had to resign from the committee because he was much too busy to attend meetings, and would Joe kindly relay this word to the members, with his regrets.

Joe felt rotten, and also keenly responsible for Shep's resignation. He lamented that the hope of the church was to gather people and not to disperse them. From the Rector's sermons, he was well aware that "church" meant "synagogue" and that in turn meant "a gathering." We gather together to ask God's blessing and to discover the riches of creative living. Bunk! We gather together to make mincemeat of guys like Shep Shallow.

These last months had been for Joe a series of meetings, reports, meetings, reports, more meetings. What in God's name did it all mean? Did it serve any great purpose if it meant alienating the Shep Shallows of the world, just so the Rodney Rams could sharpen what they thought were rapier tongues? Was it all business, administration, management theory, vested interests, group dynamics? If that was all it was, well, who needed it?

Joe tried his best to hide his feelings through dinner, but

later, when Betty was showing the Rector's wife her latest dress design, he and the Rector had another cup of coffee in the den, and they talked about the mysteries of membership.

"Joe, the Bishop says you're doing a fine job with the Stewardship Committee."

Joe smiled and took another swallow of coffee. "So that's what you heard, eh?"

"Yes," the Rector answered. "And you were a kind of experiment, you know." The Rector went on to tell Joe that the Bishop and he had talked about Joe two months before he was asked to chair the Every Member Canvass drive at the parish.

"Why me?" Joe asked with a mixture of annoyance and curiosity.

"Why not you?" was the Rector's answer. He went on to say that the church had a lot of talent which normally went untapped; or, if tapped, often for the wrong tasks or for the wrong reasons. "Let us assume," he continued, "that the Episcopal Church means well as an organization, and that it wants to provide a genuine mission and ministry within all sorts and conditions of culture. To do this well, it needs structure and people."

"The two great variables within culture?"

"Right, Joe, they are always changing and, therefore, it could be said that the Episcopal Church, as an organization, is always in flux. As such, it must develop new people to work within its ever renewed structure."

"Ever renewed?"

"Yes, by the grace of God it is always being renewed, as God deals with the likes of you and me."

"What do you mean?"

"I'm not completely sure," the Rector confessed. "In part this, though: the church, as the Body of Christ, cannot and will not fail; but the church, in its everyday sense, stumbles over all sorts of private motives and hidden agendas, because the church consists of the likes of you and me. And what are we but imperfect people attempting to respond to a perfect God. Almost hopeless, isn't it?"

Joe exclaimed that it was more than hopeless, it was dangerous. Joe felt inadequate to chair these committees, and it was more than false modesty. It was fear, fear of hurting people's feelings, fear of getting the wrong things done, fear of coming on too strong, fear of being sacrilegious, fear of not being liked, a fear of shattering failure.

"Join the club," the Rector said as he poured himself another cup of coffee. "To be a leader, and you surely have leadership qualities, means to accept the reality of failure at all times. That's why those of us who are thrust into leadership positions develop the toughest of skins and the humblest of hearts. We have to live with the fact that each day we are very likely to fail at least once, and usually that once is a beaut! But that doesn't mean we stop trying and just pack it in; no, it means that we learn from the mistakes and press on."

"Onward and upward!"

"Ah, if it only were, all the time," the Rector answered.

"Well," Joe continued, "I still recall my thoughts as I walked into our parish house for the first meeting way back about a million years ago. It was verbose, but I could summarize the essentials now: If I were to do anything of value for at least one person or one group, I would have to subscribe to the notion that I, as leader, strengthened with the traits, characteristics and principles of leadership, could put into action the proper means, which were the play and interplay of specifics, so the participants, whoever they were, would understand and respond for the purpose of accomplishing the goal, with the greatest effectiveness, with the minimum of confusion, and with the maximum of charity. . . . How's that for a mouthful?"

The Rector smiled, and then said, "Joe, what is the member's role in all this? What should be expected of Shep Shallow and Rodney Ram, Angie Angry, Curt Conflict, and the rest of them?"

The two men made some guesses about the motives and agendas of these people. Maybe Angie Angry used the church as her personal punching bag. Perhaps Curt Conflict used it to try out some of the advertising schemes his boses rejected at the office. As for Shep Shallow, who knows—perhaps he was seeking a simple way of life in the church to contrast with the complex world in which he had to operate. And Rodney Ram might delight in seeking out organizations which welcomed the Shep Shallows of the world, just so he could flex some muscles which he didn't get a chance to use too often. Who knows? Who knows indeed?

The Rector and Joe knew it was impossible, if not theologically rude, to judge the motives of any fellow Christian, but it was important for them to get a handle on something basic to them all. All of them, including Joe and the Rector, wanted satisfaction in their church work. The reasons for this satisfaction were many, but they surely included, "achievement, recognition, responsibility, growth,"[51] and all other things necessary for personal fulfillment. The hope of organizational life and work was to make it all happen with style, grace and goodwill. And congeniality.

Congeniality, like the art of communication itself, was a two-way dynamic. It was best served, Joe and the Rector reminded themselves, when three aspirations were held in proper tension: to accomplish the task at hand, to maintain healthy group relationships, and to meet the specific needs of the individual.

Joe reached for another cup of coffee but found none left. He lifted his empty cup as if to give a toast. "I fear," Joe said, "that some of my comments were as empty as this; but, nevertheless, it was good to be able to talk about them with you."

"Thank you," answered the Rector. "I don't always get the

chance to talk this way with parishioners, and it is vital that I do. Thank *you*. I wonder if it would be useful to speak as directly with Shep Shallow—and the others. We think we have him all figured out, but of course, we don't."

"That's right," added Joe. "Perhaps it is because the church, in some kind of frenzy, is trying so hard to develop new talent, as it were, that it fails to make sure the older members are nurtured and made ever new."

"Neat point, Joe." The Rector and Joe got up as their wives reappeared. "We so-called leaders are very good about taking our members for granted." He looked at the ladies.

"Does that include us," asked Betty, "who somehow get left in the sewing room while the men talk shop?"

"Whoops, sorry my dear," said Joe as he put his arm around his wife. "We were engaging in those verbal ramblings known as the coffee break, where, who knows, an occasional truth sneaks in."

"Which," concluded the Rector," should give us hope; and that is something we can talk about further . . . after the convention."

THE CONVENTION

A Diocesan Convention occurred whenever churchpeople needed to gather for a common purpose. It was normally held on the same day each year; and its business usually consisted of the election of officers plus committee and commission members as prescribed by its own Diocesan Canons. Usually the Diocesan Convention initiated or endorsed the program and budget for the following year. It was "the scene of the legislative and deliberative activity of the diocese."[52]

A Diocesan Convention was the church at work. In the

process of taking care of all the necessary items of ecclesiastical business, the convention provided the atmosphere of a family gathering, and a holy one at that. The church was the body of which Jesus the Christ was the unquestioned head, and where all baptized persons were the members. The church was thought of as *one*, because it was one body under one head; *holy*, because the Holy Spirit encompassed it, and therefore, sanctified its members; and it was *catholic*, because it was universal, holding earnestly the faith for all time, in all countries, and for all people; and it was sent to preach the gospel to the whole world,[53] territory and people, which included, of course, the far reaches of this particular diocese.

The convention began on a cold morning in November with the celebration of the Holy Communion in the cathedral, for the purpose of gathering the members to receive the spiritual strength and refreshment of God.

Joe Joiner, a delegate from his parish as well as chairman of the Stewardship Committee, slipped into a pew ten rows from the front of the sanctuary shortly before the start of the Eucharist. As was his custom lately, he read from the Book of Common Prayer as his way of shifting his attention from mimeographed reports to the sacrament which, he hoped, would be locked into his soul. He opened the Book of Common Prayer and began reading: "It is required of those who come to the Lord's Supper to examine themselves, whether they repent them truly of their former sins, with steadfast purpose to lead a new life; to have a lively faith in God's mercy through Christ, with a thankful remembrance of his death; and to be in charity with all men."[54] Joe prayed with hope, knowing that his plenitude—if he dared to hope for so much—came from God, a source somewhere beyond his reason.

Identity

The debate concerning the program and budget was shorter than in years past, because no member of the convention had been taken by surprise. Each person had received a report weeks before, and had attended at least one of the regional meetings.

One key program emerged. It was a revamped approach to the narcotics ministry. The earlier report, though well con-

---

Table 7
ASSUMPTIONS OF THE CHURCH
FROM WHICH THE DIOCESE OPERATES

Identity of the Church

Theological: The church is the body of Christ.
Psychological: The church is a focus of the Holy Spirit working in individual persons and in the community of the faithful.
Educational: The church is an agency which endeavors within the process of human development to stimulate the growing awareness of the continuing presence and activity of God among men.
Historical: The church is its history and tradition, including creeds, apostolic orders, liturgy, and Scriptures.
Sociological: The church is a human community, subject to the problems experienced by other organizations.

The Work of the Church

Administering the sacraments.
Developing the life of the parish community: A fellowship with mutual concerns both within and outside its membership.
Preaching: Bringing together the Word of God and life's experience to provide insight about God's action in the world.
Teaching: A guided, disciplined process of inquiry and discovery about the ways of God among men.
Ministering: An active, mutual caring for one another.

ceived, was too arcane, and therefore over the heads of the very people who needed to be involved in it. This new approach called for simple language, and simpler directions whereby an ever increasing number of persons could take an active part.

The program to deal with the narcotics problems in the diocese was called Operation Cooperation, to the singular delight of Stacey Status who first thought of the name, as well as members of the Stewardship Committee who had used it as their unofficial slogan. Now this specific program had won for itself a sobriquet—OC, and even Oh See, as it would be referred to in months to come—and everyone seemed pleased.

The narcotics program was specific only inasmuch as it was the larger perspective of the general work of the church itself. The Diocesan Council had prepared a breakdown of assumptions which it had taken from another diocese. (See Table 7.)[55]

The Assumptions of the Church was distributed to the members of the Diocesan Convention early enough in the day so considerable attention could be given to it. This pleased the delegates, especially those who had for years felt that the convention should be an occasion for the discovery of what it really meant to be a part of the diocese; that is, what is meant to be actively involved within that family known as the Episcopal Church. The diocese here would discover its own meanings for itself.

Cooperation

The Bishop's message to the convention took a different tack from previous years. For one thing, he used notes he had shared with Joe Joiner and Stacey Status when the three of them had met at the Downtown Club earlier in the year.

The text of the Bishop's message reflected his growing concern for *motivating cooperation* within the diocesan family. "The Bishop as leader," he said, "is what the diocese as leader should be. The individual and the organization have, as it were a shared identity." The Bishop developed ten points as guides for this leadership. In summary they were:

1. Establish goals.
2. Communicate understanding of these goals to the persons involved.
3. Justify the effort and response requested.
4. Provide a roadmap to these goals.
5. Set resources into motion.
6. Keep oriented toward the goal.
7. Provide enthusiasm, answers, and lead position.
8. Evaluate and improve.
9. Recognize and command progress.
10. Reward goal achievement appropriately.[56]

The Bishop then went on to say that he hoped the diocese would grow in numbers and in strength. But, in doing so, he also hoped it would not lose the sense of family which he felt was becoming more evident.

There was, as his studies had revealed, a great danger in large organizations such as a diocese. The larger the diocese, for instance, the less the Bishop's interest in an individual member's ideas; and the less the interest of the Diocesan Council and officers in these ideas, too. The larger the diocese, the more easily it failed fully to use the available human resources. The stimulating give and take of cooperation among Bishop, Diocesan Council, officers, and parishioners in general tended to decrease in direct ratio to the increase in the size of the diocese.[57]

The Bishop then moved on to the subject of family. He liked what had happened in this convention; particularly the fact that so much work had been done beforehand and by a larger number of people than ever before. He thanked the members of the Stewardship Committee, by name, as well as the others who had done their share to personalize the details of the program and budget, which included the Diocesan Council and its chairman. The family life of the diocese, he explained, should find its source right here in the Diocesan Convention as all its members were related to each other in the faith, and surely in the program that would make this faith come alive in community.

Trust

The Bishop concluded his message with a statement about trust in the family. "When I said the creed earlier this morning at the Holy Communion," he explained, "that meant, as someone wrote, that 'we trust He will reveal to us what He wants us to know. We cannot ransack the Creed and hope to carry off any booty. When we try to lay violent hands upon God's truth it eludes us. When we open our minds to receive at His hands it is given to us, good measure and running over.'[58]

"The same is true," the Bishop continued, "of individual members, each with an idea about the life and work of the diocese. What I mean is," the Bishop continued, "each member of this diocese has something to say, something which is very personal and real to him or to her, something which speaks of truth as that person sees it. It becomes part of the system in which we engage to do the work of the church. We cannot ransack the person or do violence to the system unless we want it to collapse and die. We have to take the chance, to accept and to love one another, to respect the system to which we give allegiance. Unless we must minister to one another, we become estranged from one another. And that," the Bishop concluded, "is, perhaps, what trust in this diocese is all about."

Adjournment

Later, as the delegates were leaving, Joe saw the Bishop, with his back to the wall, listening to a young man. The Bishop noticed Joe and motioned him over—and before the young man could start another of his marathon sentences, the Bishop introduced him as Ed Eager, a newly confirmed member of a mission some fifty miles away who wanted very much to sit in on the Stewardship Committee as it continued its work. Joe was agreeable to having Ed join them.

Joe thanked the Bishop for his message, saying that it had epitomized and capped all that the process attempted to do. The Bishop was grateful for the compliment, and reminded Joe that what he had said in his message to the convention took on more meaning because of the trust engendered by the process of building the program and budget as thoroughly as had been done. Joe, in turn, thanked the Bishop for his compliment.

Joe left Cathedral House with Ed Eager, who opened all the doors for the two of them and never stopped talking, mostly about himself and how wonderful he thought it was going to be working with the committee, especially since the Bishop himself thought so highly of it.

"Boy," Ed continued, "you must be really in with the number one man, eh?"

"Seems that way," was all Joe answered as he walked past Ed out of the building and into the parking lot. He was doing a lot of thinking, however, about why he was saddled with this brash young man, but also why the Bishop had to speak so eloquently about trust. Trust, trust, take the time to trust and to learn. Joe's thoughts were interrupted when he spotted Stacey Status and Carrie Careful near Carrie's car.

Joe introduced Ed Eager as the newest member of the Stewardship Committee, as requested by the Bishop, and suggested that the ladies might be able to bring Ed up to date about the next meeting. Joe was in a hurry and had to leave.

"Did you hear about the feedback?" asked Stacey.

Joe had not, but it seemed that all feedback about the process and final decision about program and budget was to be forwarded to their committee—for some action on their part, it was hoped.

"Just what you need, eh?" said Ed as he opened the car door for Carrie. "No rest for the weary."

"How right you are," Joe replied, as he walked backward to his car, "but, you know, it might tell us a great deal we need to know." He nodded as a final punctuation to his opinion, and, before Ed could take issue, he was in his car driving home. He was weary, but certain this new member would keep him from prolonged rest.

CONSULTATION

Stacey Status called the meeting of the Stewardship Committee to order, one week following the Diocesan Convention. She rehearsed the twofold nature of their work on behalf of the diocese. First, *to develop a program and budget for those activities best done by the diocese rather than the local church unit*. This they had done, or at least they had tried to do it. Now they had to tackle the second task, *to assist the local church unit to do its own specific work*. For this second task, the committee was to become consultant to the local church units.

Feedback

Feedback was central to the quality of life and living. Joe reminded himself of that before attending the meeting. Notes he had made some weeks ago were pertinent now. "Feedback," he had noted, "uses a way of giving help; it was a corrective mechanism for the individual who wanted to learn how well his behavior matched his intentions, and it was a means for establishing one's identity."[59] Feedback was essential if Joe Joiner wanted to learn more about who he was.

Feedback was vital if the Stewardship Committee were to exercise its role as consultant to the local church units. And they got it: some of the delegates got their materials too late; some of those called upon to speak about specific programs were not knowledgeable enough so they misrepresented them; the committee did not understand the subtleties of local problems; the committee was probably going to become one more power group; the committee might disband too soon, thereby becoming just one more flash-in-the-pan; and where was all the information the committee had promised to send about raising money?

Joe observed that the committee was now engaging in the fourth part of the process which had been described earlier in his parish, the Four Basics of Decision Making. (See Table 5) The fourth basic was the review, via self-analysis (fed by feedback among other things), with the willingness to begin all over again. The feedback would lead them to a new beginning: *preparation*, followed by the *proposal* for action; followed by the *pursuance*, the carrying out of the plan; followed, of course, by the *perusal*, where it had all begun. Decision making was cyclical.

The feedback had indicated a need for information by the

congregations as they attempted to develop their own program and budget. The committee had learned enough from its own experiences to avoid giving pat, often irrelevant, answers to the parishes. What they could do, however, was to assist others to answer their own questions. They would, in other words, provide a consultative service.

Ed Eager had a suggestion. Now that he was a full-fledged member of the committee, he offered to do all the research for the committee and come up with a plan schedule for them by next week; a schedule, by the way, which would be complete.

Joe and the others thought of Ed as a pushy young man. But Joe also remembered the Bishop's message, and the need for acceptance and trust in one another as members of the same church family, not matter how different people might be, how seemingly officious.

"Ed, thanks for your offer," said Joe. "I think, however, that it would be more helpful to all of us if we took the necessary time to study a procedure given to us from another diocese, so we might incorporate it as our own. How do you feel about that?"

Ed Eager thought it might waste valuable time, but he would bow to the interests of the group. The others thought that was very nice of him, but did not say it in so many words. They left it to Stacey to direct their attention to an investigation of the materials they had received from another diocese.

Workshops

Two weeks later the Stewardship Committee, following a review of the materials,[60] decided that they would attempt to help the local church units in as direct a way as possible. A series of workshops would be offered in the same locations used for the regional meetings. Each workshop would last a full day, preferably a Saturday. Each would consist of a morning session devoted to building a theological base for Christian giving, and an afternoon session devoted to developing organizational skills necessary for implementing an effective stewardship program. These workshops would be a free service provided by the diocese.

Invitations to attend the workshops came from the Bishop, and he mailed them out only after consulting with the Diocesan Council in an open meeting with members of the Stewardship Committee. This way, everyone was on board, and each felt that all-vital ownership in the process.

The general outline for the workshops (see Table 8) was broad enough to allow for the development of ideas and plans from within the group itself. Its goal was to create a core of key workers who would stimulate and maintain a continuing stewardship program in the local church unit. These purposes were as follows:

1. To help bring about Christian unity and fellowship within the congregation.

2. To help people deal with their questions about the Episcopal Church, local, diocesan, national, and international.

3. To help people feel that they belong and are a vital part of the congregation.

4. To enable committed members to witness to their personal stewardship and to the stewardship of the congregation.

5. To ask for financial pledges from new members, which would represent their commitment to support the ministry of the congregation.

6. To call on delinquent pledgers, when asked to do so by the clergy, to offer them a helpful ministry from the congregation.[61]

Table 8
GENERAL OUTLINE FOR STEWARDSHIP EDUCATION WORKSHOPS

A. Morning Session (9:30–12:30) *Developing a Theological Base for Christian Giving.*
   Session 1 (9:30–10:30):
   - a) Overview of biblical teaching about giving
     1) Old Testament tithe—Law
     2) New Testament giving—Grace
   - b) Theological interpretation of biblical teaching, i.e., proportionate giving
   - c) Subjective interpretation by staff, i.e., personal witness

BREAK
   Session 2 (10:45–12:30):
   - a) Participants work in groups of 4, dealing with the following, or similar, questions:
     1) What do *you really* believe about Christian Giving?
     2) What do you think you *ought* to believe, if it is different from what you *really believe*?
     3) What changes do you anticipate making in your beliefs and practices, if any?
   - b) Total group report back and sharing

BREAK FOR LUNCH

B. Afternoon Sessions (1:30–5:00): Organizational procedures and methodologies. Opportunity to work in parish teams. Opportunity for questions and answers.
   Session 1 Organizational procedures and methodologies (1:30–3:00)
   - a) General overview of tasks to be accomplished in an effective stewardship program, which may include:
     1) established goals
     2) a descriptive plan which would include
        - specific time line and target dates
        - personnel needed and method of recruiting
        - leadership responsibilities
        - training of canvassers
        - conducting the canvass
        - wrap up and evaluation
   - b) *Shape of the Organization*—a diagrammatic and descriptive illustration of an organization design that can accomplish the above tasks
   - c) *Methodology*—a step-by-step description of how the above tasks can be accomplished

BREAK
   Session 2: (3:15–5:00) Work in parish teams, and questions and answers)
   a) Parish teams will begin to develop some preliminary plans for their back-home situation (about 45 minutes)
   b) Plenary session for questions and answers (about 30–40 minutes)
   c) PMR, verbal and informal

Local Church Units

The consultants that came from the regional workshops became available to the local church unit. After the initial contact with the congregation, an exploratory meeting was held between the consultant and the leaders of the congregation. Agreements were made about two major concerns; namely, what the consultant's services would be, and what the expectations of the persons involved would be.

What services were being offered by the consultant? They included: *Diagnosis*: discovering an accurate description of the current stewardship situation. *Planning*: developing an effective plan of action, "taking into account both the unique conditions of the local congregation and the experience of other congregations which have been involved in similar efforts." *Training*: "to design and conduct a training program for members of the congregation who will be given an opportunity to volunteer their services as canvassers." *Evaluation*: "To work with the local committee in developing an accurate description of the results of the project." *Follow-up*: "To work with the local committee in projecting an effective plan of action for succeeding years."[62]

What might the consultant expect of a particular congregation? *Of the Clergy*: "That the rector be a tither, or that he be committed to the principle of tithing as a goal and be systematically working toward that goal. *Of the Leaders*: "That the leadership of the parish accept the principle of proportionate giving, with the tithe being a minimum standard and goal for themselves, and that they be willing to commend this principle to the rest of the congregation." *Of the Vestry or Executive Committee*: "To accept the concept of proportionate giving as a model for its own stewardship of the congregation's resources." *Regarding Calls*: "That the vestry or executive committee commit itself to assuring that a personal call will be made into the home of every communicant, including a call on the rector and his family." *Of the Diocese*: "That the diocese will pay the expenses for an initial visit by the consultant to a parish, and that the congregation would then pay an agreed upon amount for any further services of the consultant."[63]

Ed Eager's comment said it all. "Fellows, if you don't get the support of the local leaders, as they say, ya ain't gonna get nothing."

"Well put," Joe responded, hoping that others would adopt his conciliatory tone toward Ed.

"Hey kid," yelled Biff Blocker from the other side of the conference table. "What do you think about tithing?"

"Me?" said Ed. "I don't think about it at all." Ed smiled broadly. "Who does?"

Rodney Ram took a jab. "Do you think we should throw the idea out then?"

"No," said Ed with assurance, "shoot 'em between the eyes with that one, but from a safe disance." Ed knew he had lost some of his audience, but he continued anyway. "Sure, there's always somebody rich enough these days to tithe. Let's go after the rich guys."

"I tithe," Bull Brown said softly.

"You?" asked Ed with wide eyes. "How . . . I mean to say, how can you er, afford to?"

"I can't afford not to," replied Bull. "My dad used to remind us that it was not what we gave to charity, but what we kept for ourselves. That's what counted. But all this is a very personal thing."

Stacey responded quickly, "I think we'd like to hear your views."

Bull Brown obliged. "It might sound corny to the rest of you, but at the early Eucharist on Sunday, that's the one I usually attend, I really mean it when I say those words, 'All things come of thee, Oh Lord, and of thine own have we given thee.' I am what God uses in this world of his. In the eyes of God I am more important than my tithe. That's my sense of dignity, and, let me add, that's why I can usually take all kinds of guff. So, it's dignity. But it's also responsibility. What am I to do with what I have? What do I owe to my people, my community, and my church? I have to ask those questions all the time. And when I ask them, I have to go back to what my father used to tell us, it's not what I give to the church, it's what I leave for myself. Ten percent is reasonable enough because it means I am leaving ninety percent for myself, and that's a lot."

Joe felt this witness gave new emphasis to the points made by his rector in the early stages of their canvass work, and he quoted them to the Stewardship Committee.

> Stewardship is a piece of that complex puzzle called the church. Stewardship is a piece of that complex life called you. Proper stewardship is a thankful response for a life being put together by God's love. Stewardship is reality. God is real and you can be too.[64]
>
> The theology of stewardship is a systematic attempt of Christian thought to clarify the significance of that divine activity

for the life of man, and to guide intelligently the response which it calls forth.[65]

Everyone turned to Ed Eager and Rodney Ram, expecting they would go at it again. Silence. The men were keeping their thoughts to themselves. Stacey moved to the second question before them.

Time Line

What would be expected from the consultant working with the congregation? Flexibility. He or she had to be able to say no when necessary, and be willing to take no from others. It was a time for self-effacement, rather than self-assertion.

The following action steps and target dates were established. First, the consultant would gather data, and prepare a thorough analysis of the present stewardship situation. Second, a decision would be made as to how many co-chairmen and workers would be needed, who would recruit them, and when they would be recruited. Third, a date for the next visit would be established for the purpose of planning the stewardship program, including a *time line of target dates* and for the training of the key personnel.[66]

There were six parts to the time line; that is, the procedures to be followed within the agreed-upon schedule.

1. Following the planning and training session for chairmen and team leaders, a third visit by the consultant would take place a few weeks later. During this period, the canvass calls would be made at the home of the clergy, chairman, and team leaders for the purpose of obtaining their pledges. The clergyman, for example, would call on the chairman, and then the chairman would, in turn, call on a team leader, and so on.

The team leaders, moreover, were responsible for recruiting a consultant/canvasser for their teams, at a ratio of one for every four families in the congregation. This recruitment was far from easy, but very essential if the process was to work.

2. The consultant was to return for training sessions in the region. During this time, the team leader would call at the home of the consultant/canvasser on his own team to receive the family's pledge. Also during this time, the publicity campaign was to be intensified.

By this time, it was hoped that at least a fourth of the congregation would have been canvassed. Usually the most significant increases in giving came from the canvass staff itself, and their responses were the key motivation for the completion of the total effort. The leaders would not be expected to ask others to do something that they had not done themselves.

3. The consultant returned, once again, to a training session, this one devoted to the mechanics of calling. Normally this training was accomplished in two sessions. The actual canvass date should be at least one week later, allowing time for the mailing of a postcard to the families concerned, telling who would call, when, and for what purpose. This initial contact by the consultant/canvasser was vital. It placed the responsibility on the family either to be at home or to allow for a change in date; or, of course, to tell the canvasser that they were not interested in having anyone call. Furthermore, the postcard softened the often distasteful appearance of a door-to-door sales campaign. Finally, the postcard set the agenda for the consultant/canvasser, thereby encouraging him to complete his particular task as expeditiously as possible.

4. A well-organized canvass could, and should, be completed in two or three hours, except in those cases where rescheduling was necessary. No canvass should extend more than one week beyond canvass day.

5. Data for an evaluation would then be mailed to the

Table 9
EVALUATION OF THE STEWARDSHIP PROGRAM, 197__

PARISH_____ CITY_____

1. What was the total number of pledging units in your congregation during the previous year? _____
2. What was the total amount pledged for the previous year? _____
3. What was the total number of potential pledging units in your congregation for this year? _____
4. How many pledges were received this year? _____
5. What was the total amount pledged this year? _____

    How many potential pledging units refused to pledge? _____

    How many potential pledging units were not contacted? _____

6. How many new pledges were received _____ Total $_____

    How many pledges were increased? _____ _____

           decreased? _____ _____

       in parish but terminated? _____ _____

7. How much did your parish pay for the services of a consultant?

             Consultant Fee $_____

             Expenses $_____

8. What were the most valuable contributions made by the consultant in your stewardship program?
9. What were your major dissatisfactions with the services provided (or not provided) by the consultant?
10. In addition to the money pledges, what other effects, if any, has this program had in the life of your congregation?
11. Other Comments . . . .

Return to: Stewardship Committee, Diocesan House

consultant, which he would complete (see Table 9), thereby reducing time and travel requirements of the consultant.

6. Finally, the congregation might decide to use the services of a consultant to plan for a continuing canvass program.

"Hey," shouted Biff Blocker as he wiped his brow, "who has the time to organize all this?"

Yes, who indeed! That led the committee into a discussion of an overview for the year, to see exactly what time problems they would have to consider. The calendar revealed a tight schedule.

January and February: complete evaluation of the previous year's performance.

March and April: contact stewardship consultants and complete plans for the fall of the current year.

April and May: contact prospective congregations interested in the consultant, and arrange for the exploratory meeting with them.

June through August: assign, on a mutually agreeable basis, consultants to work with interested congregations.

September through November: recruit and assign additional consultants for training and experience.

December: collect data, analyze, evaluate, and report on the effectiveness of the current year's campaigns.

Critique

"It sounds very thorough, and all that," remarked Biff Blocker, "but how do we know it will work in this diocese?"

Stacey had received some responses to the earlier analyses of work in progress that they had made, and she summarized them for Biff and the other members of the committee.[67]

The process, as outlined, was more "theologically sound and behaviorally satisfying, because it involved more people than in the past." Almost twenty-five percent of the families were called upon to be trained consultants. This large number created within a congregation a sense of "what we were doing rather than what was being done to us," and it included a wealth of personal witness, rather than shouts of Do this! and Do that! which normally engendered all kinds of guilt feelings and markedly less support. The outside consultant, for instance, "made a personal witness about his understanding of the meaning of stewardship in his own life and in his family's life and what their response had been, even sometimes talking about dollars and cents, always in the framework of response to God's gifts." Furthermore, "surprisingly, or perhaps not so surprisingly, this process of witnessing to one another not only produced an increased involvement of the person witnessing, but it became an instrument of conversion for persons to whom this kind of witness was made."

The summary continued: The consultants constantly used real data; that is, demonstrable accurate data, not just feelings. Each individual being trained was asked to tabulate for himself—for his own information—his real income, his actual giving (which was often less than he thought he was giving), and the true percentage of giving which that expressed. A consultant, after such training, frequently utilized this insight in his personal witness. He used this witness because, for the first time, he had confronted himself with the facts of his giving; no one did it to him.

Furthermore, everyone was contacted. "Each person who agreed to work as a consultant in the canvass had to make his own commitment in his church in the presence of another consultant before going out into the parish to make his four calls. This included the clergy and leaders. This is theologically important because no one had the right to make a witness about what God had done for him and his own response as a Christian steward until he himself had made such a response." Because everyone knew that each person in the congregation was involved in the process, the chances of the individual being willing to make a sacrificial commitment were far greater. He had the feeling of "we're all in this and I'm willing to try to do my bit."

The summary concluded by saying that "church attendance increased markedly in the months immediately following the canvass. People were not left with a bad taste concerning the canvass, as had often happened previously. The level of enthusiasm engendered in the process permeated the congregation with a new sense of joy. The financial situation of the congregation was markedly improved," and the diocese benefited too, as reported:

"Because the diocese had used this process is a fairly large percentage of churches in its jurisdiction, the over-all percentage of giving in the diocese had increased, the total amount of dollars in the budget had increased although the total communicant strength had not greatly increased, though it was thought that this would follow."

"Hey, what are we waiting for?" shouted Ed Eager. "Let's get cracking!"

It was not that the Stewardship Committee did not want to get cracking, but who would be able to coordinate all that work? Could the committee do it? Yes, if it had staff help. The recommendation of the committee, therefore, would be to hire a coordinator for this work, to be responsible to the Bishop and this committee.

Having a coordinator as staff person would allow the Stewardship Committee the opportunity to take an overview of their various tasks, not the least of which was the distribution of informational packets to the congregations as needed.

Brochures

A brochure was a handy method of providing information. Its copy was terse, to the point, and designed to answer very specific questions in the reader's mind.

But should the committee send a separate brochure for each item, such as wills, budget planning, duties of the treasurer and bookkeeper? Well, yes and no. Too many brochures would be burdensome. But trying to pack too much information into one would be self-defeating.

OVERVIEW

Joe Joiner, not unlike the Stewardship Committee itself, needed to sit back and take an overview of what he was doing and why. The leader should never lose sight of the woods as he maneuvered his way among the trees.

Joe was a joiner, and he had aligned himself with enough organizations to satisfy the requirements for school yearbooks and business résumés. But now he had not only joined the Episcopal Church, he had willingly joined in its projects.

Joe was a reluctant leader. As an architect, he could be judged on his work, and not necessarily on how he presented his work to a client, because that chore could be done by others. He preferred sitting in the next to last pew. At first, he had been more interested in leadership as a theory to be explored in the mind rather than exercised in the company of others.

Joe mistrusted his ability to deal in interpersonal relationships. He feared having to spend seventy-five percent of his time maintaining public relations and only twenty-five percent of the time doing his job. He wanted it to be the other way around. Joe constantly fought back an urge to go it alone, to do whatever had to be done in his own style and at his own pace.

Joe had a home and family which he loved dearly. It was big enough for him. Therefore, talk about "the larger family" was unacceptable to him. He resisted the notion that he had to like or to associate with people selected for him by others, or by the mere chance of church affiliation.

But Joe Joiner was also fascinated about what had happened to him in the last two years. (It *had* been two years. Where did the time go?) During these two years he had learned more about the Episcopal Church than he had ever expected to learn, and he liked it more and more. As a matter of fact, he was reading more about the church than ever before. It was a far cry from those childhood days of coloring Joseph's beard.

Joe had learned about his weaknesses, and he had offered himself, with his limitations, to the work of the church. As had the others. And out of the weaknesses had come strength. More of his reading had told him that "the grace of Christ comes to me, a sinner, through my fellow sinners. The wisdom of Christ comes to me, a fool, through my fellow fools . . . and when he and I both realize that our Lord is the only physician who can help us, then we can receive from one another. . . . in our common emptiness we all share the fullness of God."[68]

Joe had also read, for example, that "the Church is the people of God constituted as such by God's self-revealing action, and the people's responses."[69] That took him right back to his point of departure, however. The problem was people, the problem is people and, for all Joe knew, the problem would always be people. People were the pain of it all, but they were also the pleasure of it all. When things worked in the meetings,

Joe knew it came after problems were changed, by the people themselves, into opportunities. So Joe repeated a different theme; namely, that opportunity was people, that opportunity is people and, by the grace of God, that opportunity would always be people. And did you hear? Joe was using the expression "by the grace of God" as freely as others on the committee did.

Joe knew that it was high time he changed his pledge from three dollars per week to something more reasonable. He had successfully avoided this in his hectic pace to work for the committee. He was walking toward his desk, to get out his budget papers and checkbook, when Betty popped into the room.

"Joe, you got a call from the Bishop this afternoon."

"Oh? Does he want me on another committee to see how things are in Australia?"

"No, smartie," Betty answered "he wants you to go to Greenwich, Connecticut, in two weeks, to attend a meeting of the Executive Council of the Episcopal Church. . . . Do remember to take your attaché case."

B.
The General Church Program

THE EXECUTIVE COUNCIL

The Merritt Parkway exit was easy to miss, even if one drove below the speed limit, as Joe was doing. Joe had a great deal on his mind, as he exited from the parkway and turned left on Round Hill Road to take the road upward past lush trees and properties, toward Seabury House in Greenwich, Connecticut.

The Bishop had been requested to select one member of the diocese to join with a few others as observers at the next regular meeting of the Executive Council of the Episcopal Church. That meant for Joe, whom the Bishop had tapped for the job, a return to the Canons of the Church for some basic information.

In the Canons, Joe read: "There shall be an *Executive Council* whose duty it shall be to carry out the program and policies adopted by the General Convention. The Executive Council shall have charge of the unification, development, and prosecution of the Missionary, Educational, and Social Work of the Church and of such other work as may be committed to it by the General Convention."[70]

Joe saw the entrance to Seabury House. He swung his car to the left and followed the well-groomed roadway to the building itself. He parked the car between two cars from states at least five hundred miles from his own. The Executive Council, he knew, consisted of forty priests and laypersons from every area of the church; and now they were all gathered at Seabury House. The house, originally a residence for one family, was now a hostel for members of an even larger one.

Joe walked in. The large room, which opened onto a rolling landscape, was comfortably furnished to provide a number of small sitting areas. To the left was a room used as an office. And to the right was a paneled room used for a chapel. Evening Prayer was being said at the time, so Joe slipped into the last pew.

A native American from a tribe in the Dakotas was reading a lesson from the Epistle to the Romans, and Joe tried to give it his full attention although his eyes strayed to the other worshipers.

"If a man is weak in his faith you must accept him without attempting to settle doubtful points. . . . Who are you to pass judgment on someone else's servant? Whether he stands or falls is his own Master's business; and stand he will, because his Master has power to enable him to stand. . . . [He saw the Presiding Bishop sitting near the wall, and next to him, a teenager dressed in the sloppiest of dungarees.] He who respects the day has the Lord in mind in doing so, . . ." [Three middle-aged women sat in another pew, next to an oriental priest and a black layman.] For no one of us lives, and equally no one of us dies, for himself alone. If we live, we live for the Lord; and if we die, we die for the Lord. Whether therefore we live or die, we belong to the Lord. . . . [Joe had heard that the physical death of the church must precede its spiritual awakening. He hoped the church would survive at least through dinner. The grumbling in him stomach reminded him that he had not eaten lunch.] He who thus shows himself a servant of Christ is acceptable to God and approved by men. Let us then pursue the things that make for peace and build up the common life. [What did Joe know about the Indian problem, and what did he really care about it? . . . Did that black layman know that Bull Brown was the only one on the committee back in the diocese who was tithing? That was a silly question, Joe thought. Did black only think about black? Bull Brown didn't.] And may God, the source of all fortitude and all encouragement, grant that you may agree with one another after the manner of Christ Jesus, so that with one mind and one voice you may praise the God and Father of our Lord Jesus Christ. In a word, accept one another as Christ accepted us, to the glory of God."[71]

Following Evening Prayer and before dinner, Joe was introduced to the five other observers. Each received an agenda for the meetings that week, and a chart showing the Organization of the Executive Council. With the chart came a verbal briefing, about which Joe made notes.

The Executive Council, consisting of members elected by the General Convention or provinces, was accountable to the General Convention. Its assignment was to carry out the decisions of the convention, even though between conventions the Council could initiate and develop such new work as it might deem necessary. Each member of the Council was assigned to a program group, as shown on the chart, and was given the responsibility for a major facet in the work of the Council. A member of the professional staff acted as liaison with each group. The Council also had a Steering Committee, Standing Committees, and Ad Hoc and Special Committees as needed.

For several years, the Executive Council had been attempting to provide coordinated and unified services and resources in carrying out the church's program of mission, ministry, and education.

These services, specifically, were: developing closer functional relationships between the national policy and program elements and diocesan units; assisting jurisdictions to develop local leadership and resources; enabling jurisdictions to share this leadership and these resources with their neighbors; encouraging dioceses to develop interdiocesan programs of action and to work with other churches and secular agencies at regional and local levels; serving as a switchboard, which was another way of saying that the Council was trying to match needs and resources throughout the church; advising on resources for converting strategy to program in jurisdictions; and, of course, identifying, encouraging, and initiating innovative and experimental projects pertinent to lay leadership development, diocesan planning, and ecumenical action.

The Executive Council, Joe and the observers were told, was a necessary national embodiment of the Episcopal Church, which was a manifestation of the Holy Catholic Church and a member of the Anglican Communion. As such, the Council had an identity and task of its own, interdependent with and complementary to other embodiments such as dioceses and congregations; it was committed to ecumenical action and represented the Episcopal Church, in appropriate ways, in relation to other manifestations of the church and other religious traditions; it all represented the Episcopal Church, in relation to other institutions of the world; it was the Episcopal Church's principal instrument for planning and carrying out its general program and budget; and it was the Episcopal Church's principal national representative agent and spokesman with the Presiding Bishop, in the interim between meetings of the General Convention.

"Which means, it sticks its nose into everyone's business, welcome or not."

Joe Joiner turned to see who said that, and was met by a toothy smile and a hearty handshake.

"Lydia's the name," said the flaming redhead in blue cashmere. "Lydia Lib. Isn't that a gas?" She pushed her hand into Joe's. "I hear you don't like the use of the word chair*person*? Why not? What do you have against persons?"

Joe smiled back and shrugged his shoulders. His mind was on the Executive Council and its various functions.

"I don't want to be called a man," Lydia continued. "Chair*man*, vestry*man*, church*man*. Would you like to be called a *wo*man. Woe is me, chauvinist is you."

"My problem is," Joe answered, "until this moment, I hadn't given it much thought."

"Just like the rest of the world."

"Yes, I suppose so." The others were making their way to the comfortable lounge next to the chapel, and Joe wanted to join them. He did a sidestep, hoping Lydia would take the hint and walk with him into the room and out of this budding argument on misogyny. She did, and even held the door open for him. He bowed slightly as he passed her.

"You ever on the Vestry at your parish?" Joe shook his head. "Someday you will be, I'm sure of that. And you know what else I'm sure of?" Joe could hardly guess. "Someday, and not too far in the future, you're going to interview not one but a few gals for the position of rector. What do you think of that?"

"I hope they're as pretty as you."

He could tell that this answer threw the argument off center, but for Joe that's where the whole issue was at the moment, off center.

Development

Joe, Lydia, and the others took seats in the room and were given what turned out to be a trenchant analysis of expansion from within the Episcopal Church—development.

The Office of Development had been created a few years earlier as a two-year experiment. It was given "a certain amount of freedom from structural program involvement which allowed the taking of a creative idea, fleshing it out, testing it, training the leadership to take it to the field, and evaluating the results. It had the funds to support these efforts; and it also enjoyed the readiness of those committed churchmen who responded to the call when asked to serve."[72]

The Development Office determined three basic ideas about its work: (1) that the church should have a clear statement of its mission, about which there was broad, general agreement, (2) that this mission should be expressed further in specific programmatic priorities, and (3) that it was necessary to determine a just and equitable method of funding.

A massive interrogation of the Episcopal Church (involving some twenty thousand members) was conducted to get answers to three questions: (1) What needs in church and society do you think the General Church Program should attempt to meet? (2) What should the priorities be? (3) How should they be funded?

The proposal for the General Church Program was presented at the General Convention in 1973, and it reflected the opinions and conclusions gathered from the diocesan visitation, plus other studies. *The General Church Program included those activities of the Episcopal Church as agreed upon by the General Convention, supported by diocesan pledges, and administered by the Executive Council.* Something must have worked well because there was a greater sense of agreement at this Convention than in previous years. As one reporter put it, "An enlarged sense of trust replaced the tensions which featured particularly the convention at Houston. Bishops and deputies alike showed inclinations for more cooperation and less dispute."[73] The General Church Program, as proposed, was evidently something in which a majority of persons assumed genuine ownership.

The trust and congeniality established for the General Convention would not stop there. The intention of the Executive Council, Joe and the observers learned, was to move on from Louisville back into all the church. The object would be to facilitate the development of accountability of the Episcopal Church at all levels, which had to be done if support and implementation of the General Church Program was to be expected.

An adequate process of developing commitment must engage the church at every level, diocesan, congregational, and individual. The minimal definition of commitment required that individuals understand the issues, know the decisions of General Convention, and affirm the right of the General Convention to make the decisions even though the individual might disagree with some of them.

Joe Joiner listed the four factors which were crucial to developing commitment: (1) adequate information; (2) the opportunity to clarify issues and define decisions that had to be made; (3) a climate conducive to informed individual and corporate decision making; and (4) adequate, clear strategy for implementing the decisions, which included acceptance of well-understood responsibilities.

Through a series of meetings to be held with the congregations, at the Diocesan Convention, at the Special Convention, and at regional deanery gatherings, it was hoped that those sent by the Executive Council would enable dioceses themselves effectively to establish and manage these processes at all levels. Surely there were many capable persons in dioceses who would serve as design resources. A part of the consulting process should be to help the delegation identify these people.

Then the group broke for dinner, and Joe could hardly wait for the ringing of the cowbell announcing that the food was on the table.

Both the diningroom and the annex were filled, and once again Joe was reminded of the cross-cultural scope of the Episcopal Church. Spanish, Western, Southern, and Midwestern accents mingled as a group queried a delegate from Hawaii. What are you doing about a ministry to the tourists? Is your Sunday school having trouble too? How can we fight postal increases? Do you use Mite Boxes also? What, are Mite Boxes still being used? Who's the rector now? You must be kidding? What about the Green Book? The worker priest? The ordination of women?

Joe felt a gentle tap on the arm.

"You hear them!" said Lydia, who was seated at Joe's table. "The ordination of women issue is being talked about all over."

Lydia was right, it was a common and growing concern of the church. As were other matters such as Sunday school, worship, missionary giving, personnel. The church was international in scope, but the issues were forever local.

Discussion continued as they ate. Could the Executive Council help Joe or Lydia, for instance, by coming right into the diocese for a series of postconvention meetings? "Think of what it would mean," Joe speculated, "if people from the Executive Council could discuss ways to involve the diocese in implementing the decisions of the General Convention, or other plans initiated since then. All sorts of questions might arise, such as: Where did the diocesan delegation itself stand on actions already taken or expected? . . . What ideas did these delegates have about ways to carry their own convictions back into the diocese? . . . How should a diocesan-wide commitment be sought? . . . What kind of feed-in was possible to their Every Member Canvass? . . . Who would be responsible for what? . . . Could any assignments be made to members of the delegations right now? . . . What responsibilities could be assigned to existing diocesan structures? . . . Should a separate group of persons be designated to oversee any postconvention process? . . . What outside team or staff assistance would be helpful in the diocese, if any? . . . What resources would be useful, and who would prepare them? . . . What was the time schedule? . . . And how could the whole process of interdependent planning be improved between now and the next General Convention?"

"Whew! Are you finished?" asked Lydia.

"I'd better be," answered Joe, getting up from the table. "If I continue, you'll call me a real company man, won't you?"

"No," she said, riding her polemic to the bitter end. "How about company person?"

As they walked through the main room toward the west wing of Seabury House, Joe continued his line of thought. "Back home, only a handful of people know what's going on in the church at large, and what national or international programs might mean to us in direct ways. And I don't mean just some little information packet, or set of slides about the work in this or that missionary area. I mean much more . . . I'm talking about an atmosphere where things could happen continuously, not just on special occasions such as Mission Sunday or Canvass Sunday. No, it has to mean more to them—to all the members—than that."

"The way we're going, a handful of people is all that will be left in the Episcopal Church. About an eight percent decline in membership for the first three years of the seventies, and, who knows, it might get worse."

"It might," Joe reminded her, "unless we start becoming

more of a family, national and international." Joe was developing his own polemic.

Joe and Lydia followed the group who were assembling in a large room, which must have been used as a summer parlor. The room was flanked by large French doors and windows opening onto the gardens. The four rows of plain but sturdy chairs and tables ran sideways in the room, facing the south wall. Along this wall were charts, a podium, and three chairs, used by the officers of the Council. They had assembled to hear a report on finances, and Joe, as observer, sat in the last row near the press section. He was prepared to take many notes.

Funding

Funding for the General Church Program normally came from congregations that had secured pledges through appeals to their membership; from dioceses that had appealed to congregations, and thus secured pledges; and from the Executive Council, which had appealed to dioceses to secure pledges. The budget adopted by the General Convention set the total asking for the General Church Program.

The Episcopal Church was known as one of the wealthiest per member, but one of the poorest in giving. In 1971, for example, the total congregational (local church unit) income for local support was $235,400,000, or only $68.33 per member. The income from congregations allocated to the dioceses was $36,400,000. The diocesan income allocated to the General Church Program for the same year was $10,500,000, or $3.05 per member. That was a discouraging but telling report on how people regarded projects outside the congregation.

How was the church to finance the current budget? The

budget was of necessity higher than it had been the previous year because expenses were greater and commitments more extensive. Aside from long-term budget problems, there was the short-term question of how to finance the General Church Program until the next General Convention, when general budget increases might be allocated.

To attack the short-term problem first, the Executive Council had put into effect a new formula for diocesan apportionments. The base of the new formula was the Net Disposable Income for each diocese; and the plan was for each diocese's apportionment to be between three and six percent of that amount. If for example, a diocese was now paying more than six percent, its apportionment was reduced to six percent. If, however, the diocese was now paying less than three percent, its apportionment was increased to three percent. Any diocese paying between three and six percent would have its apportionment adjusted between those amounts.

The ideal situation would be for each diocese to have the same percentage of its Net Disposable Income allotted for this purpose. However, a level percentage would be unworkable if enacted all at once. The hope, therefore, was that all dioceses would accept and follow the three to six percent figure, thereby reducing the spread thereafter.[74]

Joe wondered if the Episcopal Church could be hopeful about this new system. Would the dioceses be able to fund the General Church Program? Support had gone down drastically between 1969 and 1972. Now, however, there was an upswing, a remarkable one as a matter of fact, for 1972 had been a year of turn-around.[75] From 1961 to 1971, expenses had climbed at a rate much greater than that of income. In 1972, though, income on the congregational level started to keep pace with expenditures.

The meeting ended on this note of optimism about funding. Joe recalled his slogan, *New Hope Awakes*. It awakes indeed.

The Long View

The process of decision making was the subject of conversation at the breakfast table the next morning. The Council had used the four steps of decision making all right—Preparation, Proposal, Pursuance, Perusal—and now that General Convention was past, the Council was gearing up to start all over again or, better still, continuing that which had begun.

"Are you hopeful about all this?" asked Lydia as she poured herself another cup of coffee.

"Guarded optimism," was Joe's answer. "It means," he continued, "I will have to expand my viewpoint right at the very time when I'm only beginning to understand the dynamics at the local level."

"Why bother?" Lydia countered. "Do you really think the Episcopal Church is going to survive? Don't you think its going to be engulfed by the other church denominations? Look at the recession, the galloping inflation, the growing disinterest by the youth—not to mention the fight to ordain women?"

"I don't know," answered Joe as he allowed Lydia to pour him his second cup of coffee. "I don't get to church often enough. And when I do, I see the local parish as the whole church. And, I might add, I see my particular interests as the only real interests in the church. As I expand my horizons, maybe I'll even consider the ordination of women—which, by the way, I'm still opposed to even though I can't yet give you any intelligent argument pro or con. I've never faced the issue before. As a matter of fact, I've never faced all these different kinds of people before. Just a few weeks ago I thought the one committee at the parish was all the variety I was going to find in what I always looked upon as a calm, quiet, and somewhat provincial Episcopal Church."

"Then I suppose you like this," said Lydia as she passed out copies of the Statement on Christian Mission that had been prepared by the overseas bishops. (See Table 10.)[76]

Joe read the statement. At first glance, it seemed so inclusive as to cancel itself out at every turn. But on second reading it showed itself to be broad enough to take into account the variety of outreach demanded of an international body such as the Episcopal Church. Yes, the statement seemed apropos.

"All different," Joe added, "but all members of the Episcopal Church. Strange. . . . But exciting."

Capital Fund Drive

The final briefing was about the Development Office's ideas for a capital fund drive.

Development, they were told, was understood by the Executive Council to have three purposes: *first*, to release and develop the human resources within the church; *second*, to recommend the development of methods, plans, and models to enable parishes, dioceses, the Executive Council, and the General Convention to be more effective agents of mission and service; *third*, to propose means by which the church might gather the financial resources to do its work, and to find better ways of using what it had.

The third purpose would entail taking a survey of members of the Episcopal Church to determine how income might be increased and whether an intensive campaign was advisable. Information on certain basic questions was needed.

1. Did the membership readily recognize the needs, or a major need among them, as urgent? Did they feel that these needs, or any other major need, must be met to maintain and improve the church's mission?

Table 10
CHRISTIAN MISSION

The Christian Mission Is One
- It is not faith *or* works, but both
- It is not home mission *or* overseas mission, but both
- It is not giving *or* receiving, but both
- It is not growing in personal piety *or* empowering the powerless, but both

The Christian is sent to all other men at all times and in all places, to declare by word and action the life-giving Good News of the Risen Christ.

The Christian Mission Is Eternal
Our Lord's command to go into all the world overarches all of time, reaches from Roman Empire days to the space age to all the tomorrows to come.

Yesterday's missionary barrel, today's self-determination of peoples, tomorrow's as yet unformed designs—all are Christian Mission, expressions of the infinite love of God for each of His Children.

The Christian Mission Is Unique
- Many people offer food to the hungry
- Many agencies offer economic and medical and educational help
- Many faiths offer partial remedies for life's incurable ills
- Many creeds offer a measure of understanding of the mysteries of life and death

But only the Gospel of Christ offers all of these:

- Steadfastness in the face of tragedy or oppression
- Humility stronger than any earthly power
- A loving man-to-man bond that transcends time and space
- The freedom to celebrate life, whatever one's condition
- An inexhaustible joy which grows in those who share it
- Never-failing forgiveness of sins

God intends that each Christian shall offer his brother more than an ecclesiastical pattern, he must offer a personal Saviour. If the Christian, the committed man, does not offer all of these, no one else will, because no one else can.

2. Was there a constituency, a body of people with a definite interest in the projects, with the giving ability to meet the needs?

3. Was the constituency ready to give and to work to meet the needs?

4. What steps had to be taken to stimulate the maximum interest and secure the largest financial response?

Such a fund-raising survey would offer a clear picture of the feasibility of any major campaign to gather financial resources.

Assumptions

What had the Advisory Committee for Development agreed were the basic assumptions needed for its developmental goals and strategy during the coming year or so? Well, as far as Joe understood, six very realistic items stood out among the rest:

1. The Episcopal Church needed to feel the impact of the whole world, not of just that which was most familiar, known, or comfortable. (What demands did the whole world make on the Church? Moreover, what were the theological and biblical imperatives growing out of a new look at concepts such as obedience, authority, servanthood, losing one's life in order to gain life, receiving, giving, teaching, and learning?)

2. It was the responsibility of the Executive Council, as elected leaders, to lift up the vision of the church, to call members to its task, unashamedly. The Council should challenge, should offer alternatives for response.

3. The Church had a wealth of human and financial resources which were surely equal to the task, which should be made generally available.

4. To release these resources, it was necessary to present goals and objectives clearly. It was necessary to provide a

process which would involve the maximum number and diversity of people, groups, dioceses, parishes, individuals, and Foundations.

5. The end result would be a strategy based on relations of partnership between the Executive Council and dioceses, dioceses and regions, church groups and community agencies.

6. Any new developmental process demanded tapping resources in the Church at large: theologians, scholars, design specialists, fund-raisers. It had to be a total effort by the total membership.

Joe imagined he could hear the critics now: Here come the high-pressure salesmen with their palms out. . . . The Council will push its pet projects and disregard the voices of the people in the pews. . . . Let's talk less about money and more about faith. . . . His priorities are not mine, and they never will be. . . . All this Church does is ask for money, money, money.

Joe's thoughts continued along these lines as he gathered his papers and other belongings for the trip home. . . . What had he learned? As usual, he was not certain he had it all figured out. What did the church expect from the likes of Joe Joiner? What did he expect from the church as institution? What would he do for the church? What would the church do for him? Or, put another way, what would all three million or so members of the Episcopal Church *allow God* to do for them?

C.
Impressions

A story someone had told him captured Joe Joiner's attention as he drove home from the meeting of the Executive Council. It concerned a passenger on the ill-fated *Titanic* who was given only three minutes to gather her valuables. After three precious minutes, she returned to the lifeboat not with her jewels, but with three oranges. One's sense of values altered in the face of death.

At a moment of extreme crisis, Joe thought, it was always necessary to take a close look at personal priorities. It seemed to him that in each instance when the church witnessed to God within the world a crisis arose; that was, as someone suggested, the nature of the redemptive community. The church would always be in a crisis situation.

The member, within the church, lived within a personal crisis too; that is, he had his own turning points, his moments of decision. Was he to respond to the call? Was he to seek out that which could be done only by himself? Would he have the sense to want to find how he related to parts of a family larger than himself?

Joe was his own man, he had always fought for that; but he always fought for it within the relationships with others. He found increasing self-expression and self-fulfillment the more he related to others in congeniality. Joe thought about congeniality and mutuality over and over again; they had become so important to him. The more he related to others in the pursuit of goals, the better he understood who he was.

Joe Joiner was a member of the Episcopal Church. He was sought out by the church, and the church served him. He, in turn, served the church and, in doing so, discovered more of what it meant to be a full human being, created with imagination, purpose, intelligence, destiny. He wanted to be a full human being, filled with grace so he could find his private holiness and fulfillment within the holy community which served him as he served the community, for the purpose of living out part of a holy history, to the glory of God. God help him, he had found a point of view.

What was it about those oranges?

There were always three oranges, if one was willing to look for them, and to discover the benefits they might offer. Joe had discovered something about the life and work of the local *congregation* as it seeks identity within the *diocese* to give organizational form to the *general church program*. One had led to two, which in turn, had led to three, parts of the same sustaining benefit. One without the other meant a loss of something within the structure as understood and subscribed to currently.

Joe had searched and he had found his "three oranges." Would he be able to make something of them—with care, with prudence, and with a dash of faith?

Faith was an almost impossible concept for Joe. The act of having faith meant having a *personal* conviction. At the same time, however, faith was never self-produced. It came alive in him through God, the church and its system of doing things in culture. The action of faith within the church became his own.

As he neared home, Joe recalled that penciled lifeline he and his rector had drawn so casually many months ago. With all these activities, where did he place himself now? Well, still a little past center. He still had more to do before he was through.

Joe let himself in by the back door of the house, and found his son putting away groceries in the kitchen.

"Hi, Dad," his son said, cheerfully. "Was it a good group?"

"Yes, I believe so," replied Joe as he looked into a grocery bag. "Where's Mom?"

"Oh, she'll be right back. She went to church to get materials for you. It seems the Rector wants to use those materials from the diocese in next year's Every Member Canvass. And guess who the co-chairmen are?" Joe shrugged his shoulders. "You and Mom, that's who."

Joe was surprised, but delighted to know that he and Betty would be working together on a church project. He was never much for the women's club on one night and the men's club on another, nor was he excited about trying his leadership wings alone.

"Oh," his son said as both of them started emptying the bags of groceries. "I forgot to tell you something else too. Messrs Skeptic, Verve, and Conflict have agreed to serve again. And so have Mesdames Pious, Politic, and Angry. They all said they want to try it again. Mom thought you'd be pleased."

Joe was very pleased indeed. He knew that so far they had been introduced to each other and the problems of church life in only the most superficial way. One more year together and they just might get it right this time.

"There's a new member, too."

"Who, son?"

"His name is Charlie Change. Just moved here. Mom said he told the Rector that any plan that's six months old is already obsolete, so he's offering his services. He said something about being willing to revise everything for you if necessary."

Joe banged a can of soup on the table in his annoyance. That was all he and his committee needed: someone new to break up the team just as it was clicking well. Joe wanted to work with the same people. It would be easier, much easier.

"Mom thought you'd like having a new member. And she said the Rector thought a new face on the committee might be very good."

Oh well, thought Joe, as he handled the rest of the groceries with more care, why not one more member for the committee? Why not indeed? Then Joe noticed three oranges at the bottom of the bag. He smiled and picked them up, weighing them in his hands. Then he looked at his recently confirmed son, and asked, "Would you like one?"

Notes

These footnotes are reference points to more detailed studies. They are also introductions to people: Matthew Costigan, Loren Mead, Bill Caradine, Ebert Hobbs, just a few of the creative leaders available to the church. Parts of the book, referred to by these footnotes, also illustrate some important work being done in dioceses such as Central New York, Ohio and Alabama, work which should be shared with a larger audience.

1. Loren Mead (ed.), *Parish Intervention Handbook*, Executive Council of the Episcopal Church, 815 Second Avenue, New York, N.Y. 10017. Adapted from an outline for a "Life Exercise" (Planning, Inventory, Goals) by Herb Sheppard.
2. Title I, Canon 16, *Constitution and Canons*, as agreed upon following the General Convention of 1970. Note: *The Book of Common Prayer* is the second but equally important source of information concerning membership.
3. One of the basic themes of the classic by Peter F. Drucker, *The Effective Executive* (New York: Harper & Row, 1966).
4. Cf. Robert Tannenbaum, Warren H. Schmidt, "How to Choose a Leadership Pattern," *Harvard Business Review* (May–June, 1973), pp. 162-180.
5. Cf. Howard R. Mirkin, *The Complete Fund Raising Guide*, (New York: Public Service Materials Center, 1972), p. 23.
6. Study conducted by Matthew Costigan, Assistant Treasurer, Executive Council of the Episcopal Church, New York, N.Y. 10017.

7. This theory comes from George M. Prince, "Creative Meetings through Power Sharing," *Harvard Business Review* (July–August, 1972), pp. 47-54.

8. *Ibid.*, p. 54.

9. Robert T. Golembiewski, *Renewing Organizations, the Laboratory Approach to Planned Change* (Itasca, Ill.: Peacock, 1972).

10. *Ibid.*, pp. 329-330.

11. *Ibid.*, p. 330.

12. Loren Mead, *op. cit.*

13. See the brief but comprehensive brochure, *A Covenant Plan for the Every Member Canvass*, by the Rev. W. Ebert Hobbs, Diocese of Ohio (2230 Euclid Ave., Cleveland 44115) which I have relied on extensively for my presentation. It is an excellent primer and guide.

14. Quoted from material on stewardship education prepared by the Rev. Bill C. Caradine, Diocese of Alabama (521 N. 20th, Birmingham 35203).

15. Cf. Edwin A. Briggs (ed.), *Theological Perspectives of Stewardship* (Evanston, Ill.: General Board of Laity, United Methodist Church, 1969), p. 7. An interpretation by S. Paul Schilling.

16. Cf. Richard Byfield, James P. Shaw, *Your Money and Your Church* (Garden City, N.Y.: Doubleday, 1959), p. 46.

17. For an excellent discussion of this subject, see two important books: Clyde Reid, *Groups Alive, Church Alive* (New York: Harper & Row, 1969), and Harold J. Leavitt, *Managerial Psychology* (Chicago, Ill.: University of Chicago Press, 1967), p. 260.

18. Loren Mead, *op. cit.*

19. For details about a "Parish Profile," contact the Rev. Roddey Reid, Jr., Clergy Deployment Office, 815 Second Ave., New York, N.Y. 10017.

20. Surely the meaning of Robert T. Golembiewski, *op. cit.*

21. Taken almost verbatim from the brochure by Perry L. Norton, "The Planning Process" (Executive Council of the Episcopal Church, 815 Second Ave., New York, N.Y. 10017).

22. Peter F. Drucker, *op. cit.*, p. 26.

23. Cf. results of survey taken among twenty-four church leaders and reported in Ted W. Engstrom and R. Alex Mackenzie, *Managing Your Time* (Grand Rapids, Mich.: Zondervan, 1967), p. 184.

24. Cf. Peter F. Drucker, *op. cit.*, pp. 40-47.

25. *Ibid.*, p. 44.

26. *Ibid.*, p. 45.

27. Many theorists feel that ten weeks are better. For a thorough treatment of the ten-week schedule, see the Rev. W. Ebert Hobbs, *op. cit.*; and the standard text on this subject: Othniel A. Pendleton, Jr., *New Techniques for Church Fund Raising* (New York: McGraw-Hill, 1955).

28. Based on report of the Committee on the Credentials of Parishes, Donald Read, Chairman, Diocese of Central New York (310 Montgomery, Syracuse 13202).

29. Summarized from W. Ebert Hobbs, *op. cit.*

30. From Diocese of Central New York report, cited in note 28.

31. Robert A. Tannenbaum and F. Masarik, as quoted by James D. Anderson, *To Come Alive* (New York: Harper & Row, 1973), p. 38.

32. Cf. *The Creative Role of Interpersonal Groups in the Church Today*, edited by John L. Casteel (New York: Association Press, 1968); Thomas R. Bennet, "Project Laity: Group and Social Action," p. 58.

33. John L. Casteel, *op. cit.*

34. See *Constitutions and Canons*, *op. cit.*

35. Cf. "Facts We Need to Plan Ahead," a study made for the Development Office of the Episcopal Church, 815 Second Ave., New York, N.Y. 10017 by the Church Economics Project.

36. Ted W. Engstrom and R. Alex Mackenzie, *op. cit.*, p. 61.

37. Jeremy Taylor, *The Rule and Exercises of Holy Living*, abridged by Anne Lamb (New York: Harper & Row, 1970), p. 9.

38. Cf. Ray A. Killian, *Managers Must Lead!* (New York: American Management Association, 1966), pp. 101-103.

39. *Ibid.*, p. 101.

40. *Ibid.*, p. 103.

41. Cf. the very helpful brochure, "Planning and Leadership: A SALT Working Paper in Church Management," by the Rev. Charles R. Wilson (SALT, Box 156, Kent, Washington 98031).

42. Cf. *ibid.*, p. 2.

43. *Ibid.*, p. 3.

44. Robert R. Powell, *Managing Church Business through Group Procedures* (Englewood Cliffs, N.J.: Prentice-Hall, 1964), p. 20.

45. Freely adapted from the report of the Program and Budget Committee, William A. McCartney, Chairman, Diocese of Long Island (36 Cathedral Ave., Garden City 11530).

46. Robert R. Powell, *op. cit.*, p. 133.

47. Adapted from a seminar sponsored by the Joint Strategy and Action Committee, Room 1700A, 475 Riverside Drive, New York, N.Y. 10027.

48. Adapted from Howard R. Mirkin, *op. cit.*, and George W. Harrison, *Church Fund Raising* (Englewood Cliffs, N.J.: Prentice-Hall, 1964).

49. George Harrison, *op. cit.*, p. 80.

50. *Ibid.*, p. 84.

51. Vincent S. Flowers, Charles L. Hughes, "Why Employees Stay," *Harvard Business Review* (July-August, 1973), p. 51.

52. Powell M. Dawley, *The Episcopal Church and its Work* (New York: Seabury Press, 1955), p. 135.

53. Cf. *The Book of Common Prayer*, p. 291.

54. *Ibid.*, p. 293.

55. Diocese of Central New York, *op. cit.*

56. Cf. Ray A. Killian, *op. cit.*, pp. 32-33.

57. Adapted from an analysis by Jane Likert in Rensis Likert, *New Patterns of Management* (New York: McGraw-Hill, 1961), p. 156.

58. Carroll Simcox, *Living the Creed* (New York: Morehouse Barlow, 1950), p. 5.

59. Robert T. Golembiewski, *op. cit.*, p. 206.

60. Much of the material in this section, particularly the charts, is from Stewardship Education prepared by the Rev. Bill C. Caradine for the Diocese of Alabama (521 N. 20th, Birmingham 35203).

61. *Ibid.*

62. *Ibid.*

63. *Ibid.*

64. The Rev. Bill C. Caradine, Diocese of Alabama, *op. cit.*

65. S. Paul Schilling, *op. cit.*, p. 7.

66. The Rev. Bill C. Caradine, *op. cit.*

67. Summary obtainable from the Rev. Messrs. William R. Hill and Patrick H. Sanders, Diocese of Alabama (521 N. 20th, Birmingham 35203).

68. Carroll Simcox, "Our Life in the Parish," *This Church is Ours*, ed. Howard A Johnson (New York: Seabury Press, 1958), p. 83.

69. The Rev. Albert T. Mollegen, "Our Life in the Community," in *This Church is Ours, op. cit.*

70. Title I, Canon 4, *Constitution and Canons, op. cit.*

71. From Romans 14-15, New English Bible.

72. From the "Report from the Executive Council to the 64th General Convention 71–73," Executive Council of the Episcopal Church, 815 Second Avenue, New York, N.Y. 10017.

73. "General Convention Closes," *The Living Church* magazine, November 4, 1973, p. 7.

74. "Report to General Convention 1973," *op. cit.*

75. From the 1972 Annual Report of the Executive Council of the Episcopal Church.

76. Statement on Christian Mission made by the overseas bishops, October, 1971.

94

GENERAL BOOKBINDING CO.
14NY3 340
75   4   A   6549
QUALITY CONTROL MARK